WHERE TO WATCH BIRDS IN DOÑANA

Francisco Chiclana Moreno
Jorge Garzón Gutiérrez

WHERE TO WATCH BIRDS IN DOÑANA

Cover photographs: The flooded fresh marshes, © Diego López; Glossy Ibis, © José Manuel Reyes; Purple Swamp-hen, © Herminio M. Muñiz.

Recommended bibliographical reference:

Garzón, J. and Chiclana, F., *Where to Watch Birds in Doñana.* Lynx Edicions, Barcelona (Spain), 2006.

First Edition: July 2006

© Lynx Edicions – Montseny, 8, 08193 Bellaterra, Barcelona
© texts: Jorge Garzón and Francisco Chiclana
© photographs: credited photographers.

Translation: Mike Lockwood
Author's e-mail: jgarzon@botanica.org.es

Printed by: Ingoprint, S.A.
Legal Deposit: B-32609-2006
ISBN: 84-96553-20-5
ISBN: 978-84-96553-20-0

Chiclana Moreno, Francisco
Where to Watch Birds in Doñana / Francisco Chiclana Moreno, Jorge Garzón Gutiérrez. – Bellaterra : Lynx Edicions, 2006
160 p. : il. col, map. ; 23 cm. – (Descubrir la naturaleza. Itinerarios)

ISBN: 84-96553-20-5
ISBN: 978-84-96553-20-0

1. Aves-Observación-Parque Natural Entorno de Doñana.
I. Garzón Gutiérrez, Jorge. II. Título. III. Serie.

INDEX

FOREWORD

Back in the 1950s, when the first seeds of Spanish ornithology were still being sown, there were very few Spanish birdwatchers and barely any bibliographical material in Spanish.

The noble art of birdwatching had first become popular as a pastime in Victorian Great Britain, which in those days was still a veritable cradle of civilisation, good taste and natural science. Her Majesty's subjects were responsible for sowing the seeds of ornithology in Spain, as many Britons had links with Gibraltar or with the wine trade operating out of Sanlúcar and Jerez and had discovered the wonders of sites such as Doñana and La Janda. They in turn influenced their friends and local partners and the latter, along with like-minded people from the rest of Spain, formed the Spanish Ornithological Society (SEO) in Jerez de la Frontera in 1954.

Nevertheless, these pioneering Spanish ornithologists had no books in Spanish to consult and so often referred to species by their English names.

The founding of the SEO prompted a first translation of the classic *Field Guide to the Birds of Britain and Europe* by Peterson, Mountfort and Hollom, who had carried out the famous scientific expeditions to Doñana that were splendidly narrated by the second of these three authors in *Portrait of a Wilderness* (Hutchinson and Co., London, 1958). A field guide to the birds of Spain (*Guía de Campo y el Prontuario de las Aves de España*), published by Francisco Bernis around the same time, also helped greatly in the promotion of the SEO and since that now far-off day copious written information

about birdwatching in Spain has poured off the presses, as is evident from the number of Internet sites that provide daily updates about finding birds, their habitats and their populations.

Amongst this profusion of sources we now have this book by Francisco Chiclana and Jorge Garzón, which fills a gap that has needed filling for so long. Birdwatchers visiting Doñana have long been able to visit various information centres, follow itineraries and consult species lists; however, at times it is possible to get lost in the wealth of available information if your main aim is just to find one particular species somewhere in the complex world of Doñana and its marshes.

This guide provides a total of 23 itineraries in the area between Seville, Sanlúcar, Moguer and Lebrija, and encompasses the whole of the estuary of the river Guadalquivir, its salt-marshes and area of influence; it thus goes way beyond the confines of the original hunting estate of the Dukes of Medina Sidonia – the true Coto de Doñana.

Each itinerary comes complete with a basic block of information regarding the nature of the route and the birds you are likely to see there, as well as practical details to ease access via public transport, etc.

The extent of the authors' knowledge of Doñana is made clear on every page. Both work closely with the SEO: Francisco Chiclana sits on its governing council and Jorge Garzón is the SEO's representative in Andalusia.

Guide in hand, birdwatchers will now be able to discover the Andalusian haunts of the Osprey or come across the enigmatic Long-billed Dowitcher. All in all, this is a guide that no naturalist who ventures down to the lower Guadalquivir should be without.

Javier Hidalgo
Santo Domingo, September 2005

PREFACE

Spain holds a special place in the hearts of birders across Europe and beyond. With its exotic European Bee-eaters, Rollers and Hoopoes, imposing Griffon Vultures and Great Bustards, and endangered White-headed Ducks and Spanish Imperial Eagles, it holds a mix of species found nowhere else on Earth. And no part of Spain is more synonymous with birds than Doñana, a vast wilderness of estuary, marshes, dunes, scrub and woodland in the south-west, which is home to all the above species and hundreds more. And it really is vast: at more than 500 square miles (1,300 square kilometres), this former hunting preserve is surely one of Europe's greatest sanctuaries for birds.

Like many of my generation, I first learned about Doñana and its wildlife through the writings of others. Two pioneers of their time, Guy Mountfort and Eric Hosking, brought its natural riches to international attention in the 1958 travelogue *Portrait of a Wilderness*, while years later, as Spain developed into a major tourist destination and birdwatchers started visiting in numbers, an assortment of site guides attempted to summarise Doñana's avifauna with varying degrees of success. As a young birder I pored over such accounts in anticipation of one day making a visit. But when that day finally came, many years later, I confess it was something of an anti-climax. A tortuous journey in holiday traffic up the coast from Gibraltar towards Cadiz seemed to take forever, and by the time we reached Doñana the crudely drawn maps in my books and trip reports were insufficient to guide

me to all the right places and the birds I was hoping to find (how I wished I'd had a guide like this then). I vowed to return and make a better fist of it next time.

Ten years on, when preparing for a short trip to Andalusia in June 2003, a mutual friend recommended contacting local ornithologist Jorge Garzón for advice. It turned out to be an excellent suggestion, and from the moment Jorge met me at Seville airport it was clear that we were on course for an unforgettable trip. Our itinerary took us to other parts of Andalusia as well, but I have particularly fond memories of Doñana and its marshes, where we watched breeding Glossy Ibis and Purple Heron at just a few metres' range, admired Collared Pratincoles hawking over rice paddies, counted more Purple Swamp-hens in an afternoon than I'd seen in the previous 30 years, and compared notes on soaring eagles. A request to see Common Waxbill, a naturalised but local 'exotic', resulted in superb views of a party of six of this easily missed species. But best of all, on the last evening on a sandy track in a forest of umbrella pines, was a once-in-a-lifetime highlight: a Red-necked Nightjar sitting out in the open so close you could almost touch it.

Not every visitor can have the benefit of birding with Jorge Garzón in person, but this book is surely the next best thing. The wealth of first-hand experience invested in its pages by Jorge and co-author Paco Chiclana shines through: this is clearly the most comprehensive guide ever written for showing birding visitors how to get the very best out of Doñana. Where other site guides have devoted two or three pages to Iberia's top hot-spot, Jorge and Paco have excelled with a whole book packed to the brim with information. There are no fewer than 23 individual site accounts for the most productive locations within the National Park, together with detailed seasonal advice on when and where to see 275 bird species and a wealth of other useful information. If you want to find such rare European fare as Marbled Duck, Black-shouldered Kite, Spanish Imperial Eagle, Red-knobbed Coot, Pin-tailed Sandgrouse, Lesser Short-toed Lark and Azure-winged Magpie, then this is the guide for you.

In addition to such essential facts about the area's birds, what I also find pleasing about this book is that it is a thoroughly Spanish affair – there is no substitute for local knowledge. Researched and written by experts from the area with years of experience in the field, and published by one of the country's leading specialist publishers, Lynx Edicions, A Birdwatching Guide to Doñana has also been made available in both Spanish and English – testament not only to the growth of interest in birds and the wider environment on an international scale, but also to the importance and appeal of the Doñana way beyond national borders.

Dominic Mitchell
Birdwatch Magazine Editor

INTRODUCTION

PRESENTATION

Doñana is a miniature world of its own composed of a multitude of objects, landscapes and events. No one can be failed to be moved by Doñana and all its different facets: the gorgeous sunrises over Marisma Gallega, the low incisive flight of the Hobby as it hunts amongst the Swifts, the noisy Avocets chasing each other in the marshes, the groups of Glossy Ibises following the tractors in the rice-paddies, the scream of the swifts over Veta Zorrera, the silent sunsets in Ribetehilos, the asphodels in flower in La Cascajera, great flocks of birds flying into Monte Algaida, walks through the hunting estates, the smells of the scrub and the freshness of the Atlantic below the sanddunes of El Asperillo.

All this is our Doñana, whose forests, cattle enclosures, perfectly formed dunes, broad horizons and intricate marshes of uncertain waters are deservedly recognised as one of the world's greatest cultural, human and, above all, biological treasures.

The idea of saving Doñana for the birds was first mooted back in 1952, when the naturalist José Antonio Valverde first proposed the setting up of a nature reserve. Then in 1953 Professor Francisco Bernis – along with the owners – sent a letter to the head of state asking for a halt to be put to the planting of eucalyptus trees. Next, in 1956 and 1957 Guy Mountfort and Mauricio González Díez, along with Roger Tory Peterson, Julian Huxley, Max Nicholson, Tono Valverde and others, led the famous

Doñana is famous for its sunsets   © Jesús Martín

Doñana: a sea of birds   © Francisco Chiclana

Doñana Expeditions, which were so well described by Mountfort in his book *Portrait of a Wilderness* in 1958. The international renown and protection of Doñana was thus guaranteed.

The efforts to protect Doñana also bore fruit in the form of the creation of the Sociedad Española de Ornitología (today the SEO/BirdLife) in 1954 and then the World Wildlife Fund (today WWF/Adena) in 1961. Together these organisations managed to raise sufficient funds to buy the land at the heart of the Guadalquivir marshes that are today occupied by the Doñana Biological Station.

The uncontrolled growth of land speculation along the coastline prompted the declaration of the Doñana National Park in 1969, initially covering 37,425 ha, but eventually increased to 50,720 ha by the *Ley de Doñana* in 1978. The most recent extension to the National Park took place on January 12 2004 and today this protected area covers 54,120 ha. In 1989 the area surrounding the National Park was protected as a buffer zone by the creation of a natural park covering 53,709 ha.

After years of work, these protected areas – in all well over 100,000 ha – have achieved full international recognition: Doñana became a Biosphere Reserve in 1981, a Ramsar Site in 1982, an SPA in 1988, a UNESCO World Heritage Site in 1994 and was also awarded Conservation Diplomas by the Council of Europe in 1985, 1990, 1995 and 2000.

This book is all about making the most of the changing world of Doñana. It tells you where, when and how to watch birds in Doñana, and guides you both to the more obvious creatures and to those that are seemingly not there at all. With guide, binoculars and telescope in hand, and equipped with curiosity, hope, patience, respect and a dash of luck, users of this book can hope to spend many happy hours in the field in Doñana.

GEOGRAPHICAL SITUATION

Doñana is in south-west Spain in the part of Andalusia known as 'Baja Andalucía', where it sprawls around the estuary of the river Guadalquivir and across part of three provinces: the estuary and lower left-bank of the Guadalquivir lie in Cádiz province; the lower reaches of the rivers Guadaira, Guadalquivir and Guadiamar are all in the south-west of Seville province; and the remaining areas including a large part of the Atlantic seafront of Doñana occupy most of the south-eastern third of Huelva province. The accom-

panying map locates Doñana in Andalusia, Andalusia in Spain and the Iberian Peninsula in the western Palaearctic.

The altitudinal range of Doñana is not great: the highest part of the great Asperillo dune – its highest 'peak' – reaches just 106 metres above sea-level, while Playa de Castilla and the mouth of the great river Guadalquivir are at sea-level. The marshes and the rice-paddies of the Guadalquivir are vast flat plains that, albeit far from the coast, do not rise more than 2 metres above sea-level. Even so the gentle gradient from the marshes and rice fields down to the sea suffices for water inland to drain away into the river Guadalquivir.

Doñana enjoys a Mediterranean climate, with hot dry summers and mild humid winters. Annual precipitation levels may vary significantly from one year to another; temperatures, on the other hand, are much more constant. Average annual rainfall is around 535-550 mm, although rainfall in Mediterranean climes fluctuates greatly and in

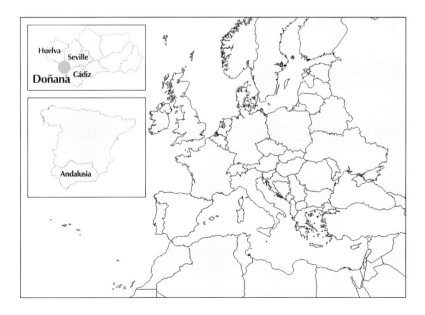

The flooded fresh marshes   © Diego López

years such as 1980 and 1994 total rainfall was no greater than 300 mm, while 900 and 1000 mm were recorded in 1987 and 1995, respectively.

GEOMORPHOLOGICAL ORIGIN OF DOÑANA

It is not a simple task to provide a summary of the formation of the Doñana, a veritable 'ecosystem full of ecosystems'. To begin we have to go back 6,000 years to when the river Betis (today the Guadalquivir) flowed into the Atlantic via an enormous gulf-shaped estuary. By the end of the Tertiary Period (Pliocene), the estuary was beginning to silt up as a result of all the mud

being washed down by the river and the sandy sediments deposited by the sea. In the Quaternary Period the amount of material deposited by the sea and by the winds began to increase and soon, coupled with a drop in sea-level, the river began to braid and flow to the sea through an intricate network of channels. Little by little a sand-bar formed across the mouth of the estuary/gulf and transformed it into a closed bay. This is how the first inhabitants of the area – the *Lacus Ligustinus* – would have found Doñana.

From here on, this huge bay continued to slowly and inexorably fill up: sand from the sea formed coastal dune systems that marched inland and cre-

The rivers and streams burst their banks in rainy years © Jorge Garzón

The marshes in mid-summer　　© Jorge Garzón

ated one of the most important ecosystems of Doñana: the dunes and sand flats.

At the same time, the river was bringing down huge amounts of mud and clay and depositing it in the bay, thereby giving birth to a second ecosystem that complements the first: the marshes with its *lucios* (permanent lagoons) and *caños* (seawater channels). A third important ecosystem is the umbrella pine (*Pinus pinea*) woodland. Despite being the commonest tree in Doñana, the origin of this tree is somewhat controversial: some claim that autochthonous stands of the species exist, while others say that it was introduced by the Romans. Be that as it may, today it is impossible to move around Doñana without coming across stands of umbrella pines, largely because from the seventeenth century onwards this tree was planted to fix the dune cordon

and prevent it spreading any further inland.

SCOPE OF THIS BOOK

This is the first book to describe all three of the provinces that form part of Doñana and provides information regarding well-known and unknown (but no less interesting) sites for birdwatchers. The itineraries are all located within the Guadalquivir marshes and its environs (routes in the restricted-access area of the National Park are not included) and these 150,000 ha of terrain include the National Park, El Lucio del Lobo, El Corredor Verde del Guadiamar, El Brazo del Este, La Corta de los Olivillos, the pinewoods of Hinojos, Aznalcázar and La Algaida, El Arroyo de la Rocina, El Charco del Acebrón, La Marisma del Rocío and Las Lagunas del Acebuche. Furthermore, we

Autumn in El Lucio del Lobo   © Diego López

describe other excellent birdwatching sites such as El Médano del Asperillo, the *montes* of Abalario and Ribetehilos, the rice-paddies of Isla Mayor and Cantarita, the Bonanza and Monte Algaida saltpans, La Carretera de Práctico, La Laguna de Tarelo, the *arroyos* of Algarbe and El Partido, the Trebujena salt-marshes, El Brazo de la Torre, Entremuros, the *dehesas* of Abajo and Pilas, La Cañada de Rianzuela, the *caños* of Guadiamar and La Vera, the beaches of Castilla and La Jara, and the mouth of the river Guadalquivir.

The itineraries pass through the following municipalities: Almonte, Hinojos, Chucena, Aznalcázar, Puebla del Río, Isla Mayor, Coria del Río, Dos Hermanas, Los Palacios y Villafranca, Utrera, Trebujena, Sanlúcar de Barrameda and Chipiona.

HOW TO GET TO DOÑANA

The Doñana area is well-communicated and the three nearby cities are all easy to reach. The city of Seville itself is the main entry point into Andalusia and is connected by a motorway, dual-carriageway, rail (including a high-speed rail connection) and an international airport.

Although the part of Doñana in Huelva province can be reached from the other towns in the area, the city of Huelva is well connected to the rest of Andalusia by motorway, main roads and rail, and is also within striking distance of Seville airport (100 km) and Faro airport (125 km) in the Algarve in Portugal.

The best city base for discovering Doñana in Cádiz province is strategically situated Jerez de la Frontera. It is connected to the rest of Andalusia by

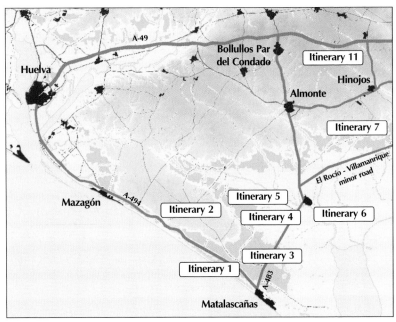

Access to the itineraries in Huelva province

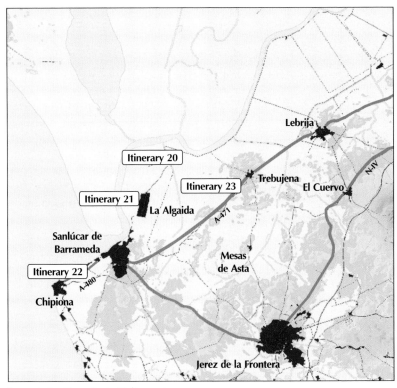

Access to the itineraries in Cádiz province

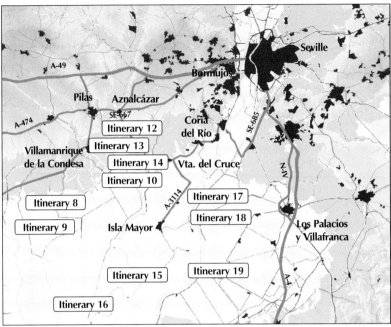

Access to the itineraries in Seville province

motorway, dual carriageway and rail, and also has an international airport.

Once arrived in one of these three cities, the main roads that will take you into Doñana are as follows:
— A-494 San Juan del Puerto-Matalascañas
— A-483 Bollullos Par del Condado-Matalascañas
— A-474 Hinojos-Seville
— Motorway A-49 Seville-Huelva
— SE-667 Aznalcázar-Isla Mayor
— A-3114 Venta del Cruce-Isla Mayor
— N-IV/A-4 Madrid-Cádiz
— SE-685 Dos Hermanas-Isla Mayor
— A-480 Sanlúcar de Barrameda-Chipiona
— A-471 Trebujena-Sanlúcar de Barrameda

Practically all the towns that appear in this guide are reachable by bus. Timetables change from summer to winter and so it is best to ask for times in the bus-stations of the three major towns. The phone numbers of the bus-stations are as follows:
— Huelva: Bus station 'Damas'. Tel.: + 34 959 256 900
http://www.damas-sa.es/buscar.htm
— Seville: Bus station 'Plaza de Armas'. Tel.: + 34 954 908 040
— Jerez de la Frontera: Central bus station. Tel.: +34 956 342 174.

Once in Doñana we recommend that you head for one of the visitor and/or interpretation centres in the National and Natural parks that have been set up in the surrounding towns and villages. The staff are always very knowledgeable and will be only too pleased to help. The telephone numbers are as follows:
Huelva province:
— Almonte
La Rocina Visitor Centre. Tel.: +34 959 442 340
El Acebrón Visitor Centre. Tel.: +34 959 506 162

The coastline, still untouched in many places   © Jorge Garzón

El Acebuche Visitor Centre. Tel.:
+34 959 448 711
SEO/BirdLife Ornithological Centre
(under construction). Tel.: +34 605
909 771
— Hinojos
Los Centenales Visitor Centre.
Parque Municipal, road from Hino-
jos to Almonte.
Seville province:
— Aznalcázar
José Antonio Valverde Visitor Cen-
tre. Tel.: +34 696 651 205
Buitrago Interpretation Centre.
— Villamanrique
Dehesa Boyal Interpretation Centre.
— Puebla del Río
Dehesa de Abajo Interpretation
Centre (under construction).
Cádiz province:
— Sánlucar de Barrameda
Fábrica de Hielo Visitor Centre.
Tel.: +34 956 381 635

HABITATS IN DOÑANA

Doñana boasts a wide-ranging mosaic
of habitats that provide for very species-rich bird communities. The following are the most important habitats in
the area.

Coast

The beaches of Doñana, bathed by the
Atlantic, are characterised by their
great inter-tidal range and fine golden
sands that in some places are inter-
mixed with pebbles and algae. The predominant wind blows from the south-
west and is known as the *foreño*; it is
the main factor in the formation of
Doñana's unique mobile dunes.

Forests and woods

Five western Mediterranean tree species predominate in the woods of
Doñana: the commonest is the umbrella (or stone) pine (*Pinus pinea*), which
was used in plantations and forms

stands known as *cotos*; wild olive trees (*Olea europaea* var. *sylvestris*) grow in important stands on the northern and western edges of the salt-marshes and rice-paddies, preferably on the most acidic soils; the cork oak (*Quercus suber*) is a denizen of the loose permeable soils that form in damp areas close to the aquifer; the holm oak (*Quercus rotundifolia*) substitutes the previous species on the drier substrata in the north and east of the area covered by this guide; and the Phoenician juniper (*Juniperus phoenicea* subsp. *turbinata*) forms stands on the coastal sands. As well, we should mention the eucalyptus plantations, now in regression, and the groves of fruit trees.

Riparian woodland
The rivers and streams of Doñana are lined with riparian forests, generally deciduous, made up essentially of narrow-leaved ash (*Fraxinus angustifolia*) and white poplar (*Populus alba*), along with other species such as elms, willows, tamarisks, dogwood, wild vine and oleander, which together form attractive gallery forests.

Marshes
These flat extensions of impermeable clays, liable to flooding, are the most important habitat in the Guadalquivir estuary. The average gradient of these shallow flooded areas is less than 0.1% and in summer, after they dry up, the clay cracks in characteristic fashion. Somewhat deeper areas of the *marismas* (marshes) where the water is more permanent are known as *lucios* and here aquatic vegetation develops and attracts diving duck. The fringing vegetation consists of a belt of helophyte plants such as sea club-rush (*Scirpus maritimus*), bulrush (*Typha* spp.), common club-rush (*Scirpus lacustris*) and *Scirpus littoralis*; in spring many *lucios* are covered by a mantle of pond water-crowfoot (*Ranunculus peltatus*).

The *caños* are channels that drain river and rain water into the flood plain and the active branches of the river. Here the vegetation basically consists of sea club-rush.

The higher areas are known as *vetas* or *paciles* and only flood very rarely. The vegetation here consists of halophyte plants such as *Arthrocnemum* spp. and shrubby sea-blite *Suaeda vera* that cannot cope with being under water for too long. These are important areas for breeding waders and other water birds and are the only places of refuge in periods of heavy rain. Once upon a time, the flooding of the marshes depended on rain, river water and the sea. Today, however, the marshes have been transformed and depend above all on the increasingly irregular rainfall to flood.

Rice-paddies
The rice-paddies substitute the marshes in much of the northern and eastern part of Doñana on both sides of the river Guadalquivir. Little of the original vegetation remains – mainly along the drainage channels and ditches and in floodable areas – and consists essentially of members of the Goosefoot family (Chenopodiaceae) and patches of common reed (*Phragmites australis*) along the banks of water courses. The rice-paddies complement the natural flood cycle of the *marismas*: when the marshes dry up in summer, the rice-paddies are flooded and birds have somewhere to feed and rest. Then, once the rice-paddies dry up at the end of summer, the autumn rains arrive and flood the marshes once again.

The characteristic rice silos   © Francisco Chiclana

Freshwater lagoons and marshland

Doñana has a full complement of lagoons (including semi-natural irrigation ponds), stretches of river and marshland of certain permanence. Although water levels tend not to be linked to those of the salt-marshes, there is often a connection between water levels in these habitats and those of the rice-paddies. The vegetation here consists mainly of subaquatic plants and belts of reeds, bulrushes and tamarisks.

Montes

The *montes* are areas of Mediterranean scrub that help stabilise the dunes. The water-table is very deep and soils are relatively humid. The *monte negro* develops in the more humid areas and

the commonest plants include heathers (*Erica* spp.), myrtle (*Myrtus communis*), *Phillyrea angustifolia* and *Daphne gnidium*. In higher areas and where the soils are drier, the so-called *monte blanco* dominates, with plants such as *Halimium halimifolium*, genistas *(Genista* spp.) and rosemary (*Rosmarinus officinalis*).

Vera

This is the transition zone between the *marisma* and the stabilised dunes and may be covered by cork oaks, scrub or pasture. The water from the areas of permanent sands help to keep the *vera* green throughout most of the year and it is a very attractive area for herbivores such as Red and Fallow Deer and Wild Boar.

Steppe

The *estepa* is the driest area in Doñana and consists of the waterless dried-out marshes and fallows, in which the predominant vegetation is annual and biannual plants.

Cultivated areas

Apart from the rice-paddies, large areas of Doñana are cultivated, the main crops being non-irrigated cereals and irrigated cotton fields and vineyards.

WHEN TO COME TO DOÑANA

Any time of year is good for visiting Doñana, although summer is perhaps the least rewarding time.

Winter, marked by the arrival of the Meadow Pipits, is always the most fascinating time for birdwatchers. The sheer quantity of water birds is a sight for sore eyes, above all in years of generous rainfall. Thousands of noisy Northern Shoveler, Pintail and Eurasian Wigeon fill the wetlands with colour and brighten up the short days of winter. Black Storks, large groups of White Storks, Greater Flamingos and Common Cranes add to the list, and raptors such as Marsh Harriers in large roosts, Merlins and Red Kites from the north, and a few Lesser Spotted and Spotted Eagles from the east add to the unforgettable feast of winter wildlife.

Spring comes early at these latitudes and begins with the arrival of breeding birds that have spent the winter in Africa. Black Kites, Long-eared Owls and Booted Eagles search for nesting sites

Bulrushes are common along many water courses © Francisco Chiclana

Water and clear blue skies in winter   © Jorge Garzón

in the umbrella pine woods, while war-blers, Purple Swamp-hen, Slender-billed Gulls, Black-winged Stilts, Collared Pratincoles and Avocets bring life to the marshes and reedbeds. The flooded rice-paddies provide food for large numbers of birds, while the Lesser Short-toed and Short-toed Larks are often seen dust-bathing along the tracks.

Summer is the dry season in Doña-na, although the few wetlands that maintain their water levels play home to Marbled Duck and Red-knobbed Coot. If spring has been generous with its rains, the heron colonies are frenet-ic with the comings and goings of the Squacco, Night and Purple Herons, Glossy Ibis and increasing numbers of Grey Heron and Eurasian Spoonbills.

Overhead you may be lucky to witness the first flights of a juvenile Spanish Imperial Eagle, while the clamour of the Gull-billed and Whiskered Terns will accompany you throughout much of the day. Summer days are long and the 16 hours of light will enable you to visit much of the Doñana, although in drought years the number of water birds will be much less.

Autumn is the time of year for migrants. Millions of hirundines and waders of all shapes and sizes provide acrobatic displays at dusk; the rice harvest and the subsequent ploughing of the paddies attracts vast numbers of birds from all over Doñana, including the Greylag Geese, whose autumnal arrival completes the yearly ornithological cycle.

TEN TIPS FOR BIRDWATCHING IN DOÑANA

1. Be patient and quiet. Try to always go out in small groups to avoid disturbing the birds.

2. The best times of day for birdwatching are the early morning and/or the last few hours of the afternoon/evening. In winter when temperatures are low, birds are most active a couple of hours after sunrise once the sun has warmed the air a little.

3. Birds are a part of the landscape and so try and enjoy the birds you see in the context of their surroundings.

4. Respect the environment and all the plant and animal species you come across. The needs of a bird must be put before your desire to see it, above all if it is rare or threatened. Never disturb birds, especially during the breeding season.

5. Distances in Doñana are large, although they may not seem so at first. Before heading into the maze of tracks by vehicle, check to see if you have enough fuel.

Ploughing the rice-paddies   © Daniel López Huertas

A common scene during migration periods   © Diego López

6. A mobile phone (even if it is not turned on) may come in handy in case of accident or any other misfortune. There is sufficient network cover throughout most of the area.

7. Always carry a map (see the notes at the beginning of each itinerary) as the maps in this guide only provide a general idea of the terrain you will encounter. Carry a bird-guide to be able to identify the species you see correctly.

8. A normal car will take you to many places in Doñana, although a four-wheel drive vehicle will be a boon in rainy years. If after rain some of the tracks become impassable, turn back and look for an alternative. Also take extra care when driving along sandy tracks.

9. Although temperatures rarely drop below freezing, in winter the humidity will increase the sensation of cold. In summer, however, temperatures can reach over 40°C at midday and you must wear a hat and suncream.

10. Long-sleeved clothing and insect repellent are essential in the early evening.

USE OF THIS GUIDE

This guide aims to make it possible for readers to see most of the 288 basic species of bird that frequent the natural paradise of Doñana. We hope that you will get to know the whole area of the marshes and estuary of the river Guadalquivir through the birds.

In all, 23 itineraries are described. At the beginning a table gives you all the basic information of the route: UTM coordinates of the start and end points, total distance, appropriate maps and the municipalities you cross. Then, after a brief introduction, the text suggests (in most cases) a series of stopping-points for observing certain species of birds. As well, you will find a map and various photographs of the most typical species of the area and of the landscape. At the end, there is a list of practical recommendations and access details for wheelchair users. We strongly recommend that you read all the details before setting off.

All the itineraries are flexible and can be changed or altered as visitors wish. Specific birds can be seen best where this guide indicates, although this does not mean that they will not appear elsewhere. At the end two tables summarise the information in the book: one lists the details of each itinerary, with the coordinates of the beginning and end points, the distance (on foot and by car), the natural habitats it visits and the province(s) it passes through.

The other table consist of a list of the 288 species of bird mentioned in this guide, with details regarding their status and abundance and on which itineraries they can be observed. This table is a useful guide for finding the appropriate itinerary and time of year for a particular species and includes breeding birds, migrants and winter visitors, as well as rare and accidental species that are recorded more or less regularly or were first recorded in Doñana.

The meaning of the abbreviations in the column 'Status' in the table of the birds of Doñana is as follows:

Abreviation	Status	Definition
Acc	Accidental	A species that appears occasionally in the area, but which is not part of the established bird communities of Doñana.
B	Common breeder	A species that is a widepsread breeder in the area.
b	Rare breeder	A species that is a localised breeder in the area.
M	Common migrant	A species that is commonly seen during migration periods.
m	Rare migrant	A species that is only seen rarely during migration periods.
W	Common winter visitor	A species that is a common winter visitor.
w	Rare winter visitor	A species that is a rare winter visitor.

The systematic bird list is based on the *Lista de las aves de España*, published in 2005 by SEO/BirdLife. We recommend that you follow the itineraries in a relaxed fashion, although the final decision as to how fast or slow you go will depend on you. All the itineraries can be completed in a day, although some are quite long and you may want to split them up into a number of different parts.

KEY

The maps that accompany every itinerary have been drawn from digital aerial photographs of Andalusia published by the Ministry of the Environment of the Andalusian Government. A series of signs, lines and colours on the maps indicate the following features:

- ⅏ Scrub, low vegetation.
- 🌴 Pine woodland, conifer plantations.
- 🌴 Isolated pine or open pine *dehesa*.
- 🌴 Eucalyptus.
- 🌴 Deciduous trees, tamarisks.
- 🌴 *Dehesa*, isolated deciduous trees.
- 🄷 Observation point. Stopping point on itinerary.
- • Start of itinerary.
- 🅿 Car-park or place to leave vehicle.
- 🄽 Visitor centre. Information centre.
- 🄽 Hide, observation point. Hut.
- 🢑 Farm. Houses. Town or village.
- ═ Asphalted road.
- — Itinerary with vehicle.
- ⋯ Itinerary on foot.
- 🄸 Lighthouse.
- Exotic plant species. Eucalyptus plantations.
- Marshland, tamarisks, deciduous woodland. Riparian woodland.
- Scrub, low vegetation.
- Dry marshes.
- 🄲 Floodable marshland. Canals and tidal channels.

RECOMMENDED READING

Chiclana, F., Lama, J. A. y Salcedo, J. 2002. *Aves de la provincia de Sevilla: comentarios sobre estatus, fenología, hábitat y distribución.* Diputación Provincial de Sevilla y Sociedad Española de Ornitología. Sevilla.

De Ceballos, B. y Ojea, A. 2005. *Guía de campo de las aves de Doñana.* Fundación Doñana 21. Almonte (Huelva).

Equipo de Seguimiento de Procesos Naturales. Estación Biológica de Doñana-CSIC. 2004. *Anuario Ornitológico de Doñana, núm. 1, Septiembre 1999-Agosto 2001.* Estación Biológica de Doñana y Ayuntamiento de Almonte. Almonte (Huelva).

García, L., Ibáñez, F., Garrido, H., Arroyo, J. L., Máñez, M., Calderón, J. 2000. *Prontuario de las Aves de Doñana. Anuario Ornitológico de Doñana, núm. 0.* Estación Biológica de Doñana y Ayuntamiento de Almonte. Almonte (Huelva).

Garrido, H. 2000. *Palabrero de Doñana, Introducción al léxico tradicional de las Marismas del Guadalquivir.* Editorial Rueda. Madrid.

Jacoby, M. 2002. *A Day in Doñana.* Martin Jacoby Editor. Málaga.

Ruiz de Larramendi, A. (coord.) 2002. *Guía de visita del Parque Nacional de Doñana.* Organismo Autónomo Parques Nacionales, MIMAM. Madrid.

Varios autores. 2002. *Parque Nacional de Doñana.* Ministerio de Medio Ambiente y Canseco Editores. Talavera de la Reina (Toledo).

SYSTEMATIC LIST OF BIRDS MENTIONED IN THIS BOOK AND WHERE TO FIND THEM

ENGLISH NAME	LATIN NAME	SPANISH NAME	Status	ITINERARY
ANATIDAE				
Mute Swan	Cygnus olor	Cisne Vulgar	Acc	14
Bean Goose	Anser fabalis	Ánsar Campestre	m–w	6
Pink-footed Goose	Anser brachyrhynchus	Ánsar Piquicorto	m–w	8
White-fronted Goose	Anser albifrons	Ánsar Careto	m–w	8–9–15
Lesser White-fronted Goose	Anser erythropus	Ánsar Chico	m–w	15
Greylag Goose	Anser anser	Ánsar Común	M–W	6–8–9–10–14–15
Snow Goose	Anser caerulescens	Ánsar Nival	m–w	9
Bar-headed Goose	Anser indicus	Ánsar Indio	m–w	9
Canada Goose	Branta canadensis	Barnacla Canadiense	m–w	9–15
Barnacle Goose	Branta leucopsis	Barnacla Cariblanca	m–w	8–9–15
Brent Goose	Branta bernicla	Barnacla Carinegra	m–w	9
Egyptian Goose	Alopochen aegyptiaca	Ganso del Nilo	Acc	10
Ruddy Shelduck	Tadorna ferruginea	Tarro Canelo	Acc	8–15
Common Shelduck	Tadorna tadorna	Tarro Blanco	b–M–W	6–20–21
Eurasian Wigeon	Anas penelope	Silbón Europeo	M–W	3–6–8–9–17
American Wigeon	Anas americana	Silbón Americano	Acc	9
Gadwall	Anas strepera	Ánade Friso	B–M–W	3–4–8–10–13–17
Common Teal	Anas crecca	Cerceta Común	M–W	3–4–8–10–14–19
Mallard	Anas platyrhynchos	Ánade Azulón	B–M–W	4–7–8–10–13–17
Pintail	Anas acuta	Ánade Rabudo	M–W	3–6–8–9–17–21
Garganey	Anas querquedula	Cerceta Carretona	M	4–10–14–19
Northern Shoveler	Anas clypeata	Cuchara Común	M–W	3–4–8–9–14–17
Marbled Duck	Marmaronetta angustirostris	Cerceta Pardilla	b–m–w	9–10–14–18–19–20
Red-crested Pochard	Netta rufina	Pato Colorado	B–M–W	3–4–8–13–17–21
Common Pochard	Aythya ferina	Porrón Europeo	B–M–W	3–4–8–14–17–21
Ferruginous Duck	Aythya nyroca	Porrón Pardo	m–w	3
Tufted Duck	Aythya fuligula	Porrón Moñudo	M–W	13–17–21
Greater Scaup	Aythya marila	Porrón Bastardo	m–w	17
Common Scoter	Melanitta nigra	Negrón Común	M–W	1–22
Ruddy Duck	Oxyura jamaicensis	Malvasía Canela	Acc	17
White-headed Duck	Oxyura leucocephala	Malvasía Cabeciblanca	b–m–w	17–20–21
PHASIANIDAE				
Red-legged Partridge	Alectoris rufa	Perdiz Roja	B–M–W	2–3–7–18–23
Quail	Coturnix coturnix	Codorniz Común	B–M–w	7–11–12–18–23
GAVIIDAE				
Red-throated Diver	Gavia stellata	Colimbo Chico	m–w	1
Great Northern Diver	Gavia immer	Colimbo Grande	m–w	1

ENGLISH NAME	LATIN NAME	SPANISH NAME	Status	ITINERARY
	PODICIPEDIDAE			
Little Grebe	*Tachybaptus ruficollis*	Zampullín Común	B–M–W	3–8–10–14–19–20
Great Crested Grebe	*Podiceps cristatus*	Somormujo Lavanco	B–M–W	3–8–13–17–19
Black-necked Grebe	*Podiceps nigricollis*	Zampullín Cuellinegro	B–M–W	8–14–17–20–21
	PROCELLARIIDAE			
Cory's Shearwater	*Calonectris diomedea*	Pardela Cenicienta	M–W	1–22
Balearic Shearwater	*Puffinus mauretanicus*	Pardela Balear	M–W	1–22
	HYDROBATIDAE			
European Storm-petrel	*Hydrobates pelagicus*	Paíño Europeo	m–w	22
Leach's Storm-petrel	*Oceanodroma leucorhoa*	Paíño Boreal	m–w	22
	SULIDAE			
Northern Gannet	*Morus bassanus*	Alcatraz Atlántico	M–W	1–22
	PHALACROCORACIDAE			
Great Cormorant	*Phalacrocorax carbo*	Cormorán Grande	M–W	8–9–10--13–16
	PELECANIDAE			
White Pelican	*Pelecanus onocrotalus*	Pelícano Común	Acc	8
	ARDEIDAE			
Great Bittern	*Botaurus stellaris*	Avetoro Común	b–m–w	9–13–19
Little Bittern	*Ixobrychus minutus*	Avetorillo Común	B–M	3–6–9–10–18–19
Night Heron	*Nycticorax nycticorax*	Martinete Común	B–M–W	7–8–14–16–17–19
Squacco Heron	*Ardeola ralloides*	Garcilla Cangrejera	B–M–w	6–9–10–17–18–19
Cattle Egret	*Bubulcus ibis*	Garcilla Bueyera	B–M–W	6–7–13–15–17–19
Western Reef Heron	*Egretta gularis*	Garceta Dimorfa	Acc	16–17
Little Egret	*Egretta garzetta*	Garceta Común	B–M–W	8–10–14–15–17–19
Great Egret	*Egretta alba*	Garceta Grande	m–w	8–14–15–19–20
Grey Heron	*Ardea cinerea*	Garza Real	b–M–W	7–8–13–15–17–20
Purple Heron	*Ardea purpurea*	Garza Imperial	B–M	3–9–10–15–16–19
	CICONIIDAE			
Black Stork	*Ciconia nigra*	Cigüeña Negra	M–W	8–14–15–18–19
White Stork	*Ciconia ciconia*	Cigüeña Blanca	B–M–W	7–9–14–15–16–18
Yellow-billed Stork	*Mycteria ibis*	Tántalo Africano	Acc	16
Marabou Stork	*Leptoptilos crumeniferus*	Marabú Africano	Acc	8
	THRESKIORNITHIDAE			
Glossy Ibis	*Plegadis falcinellus*	Morito Común	B–M–W	4–8–9–10–15–17
Sacred Ibis	*Threskiornis aethiopica*	Ibis Sagrado	Acc	17
Eurasian Spoonbill	*Platalea leucorodia*	Espátula Común	b–M–W	6–8–14–18–19–20
African Spoonbill	*Platalea alba*	Espátula Africana	Acc	8–18

ENGLISH NAME	LATIN NAME	SPANISH NAME	Status	ITINERARY
PHOENICOPTERIDAE				
Greater Flamingo	Phoenicopterus roseus	Flamenco Común	b–M–W	6–9–10–18–20–21
Lesser Flamingo	Phoenicopterus minor	Flamenco Enano	Acc	9
ACCIPITRIDAE				
Black-shouldered Kite	Elanus caeruleus	Elanio Común	b–m–w	3–4–11–13–14
Black Kite	Milvus migrans	Milano Negro	B–M	6–12–13–14–16–21
Red Kite	Milvus milvus	Milano Real	m–w	2–6--8–21
Egyptian Vulture	Neophron percnopterus	Alimoche Común	M	6–9
Griffon Vulture	Gyps fulvus	Buitre Leonado	M–W	6–9
Short-toed Eagle	Circaetus gallicus	Culebrera Europea	b–M	8–12–16–21
Marsh Harrier	Circus aeruginosus	Aguilucho Lagunero Occidental	B–M–W	7–9–10–16–17–19
Hen Harrier	Circus cyaneus	Aguilucho Pálido	M–W	8–9–13–16–19
Montagu's Harrier	Circus pygargus	Aguilucho Cenizo	B–M	8–10–13–17–23
Northern Goshawk	Accipiter gentilis	Azor Común	b–m–w	5–13
Sparrowhawk	Accipiter nisus	Gavilán Común	b–M–W	2–5–12–17
Common Buzzard	Buteo buteo	Busardo Ratonero	B–M–W	6–8–11–12–16–23
Long-legged Buzzard	Buteo rufinus	Busardo Moro	Acc	9
Lesser Spotted Eagle	Aquila pomarina	Águila Pomerana	m–w	6
Spotted Eagle	Aquila clanga	Águila Moteada	m–w	4
Spanish Imperial Eagle	Aquila adalberti	Águila Imperial Ibérica	b–m–w	2–6–9–16–20
Booted Eagle	Hieraaetus pennatus	Aguililla Calzada	B–M–w	2–4–12–14–17–18
PANDIONIDAE				
Osprey	Pandion haliaetus	Águila Pescadora	M–W	13–15–16–17–20
FALCONIDAE				
Lesser Kestrel	Falco naumanni	Cernícalo Primilla	b–m–w	16–20
Common Kestrel	Falco tinnunculus	Cernícalo Vulgar	B–M–W	2–12–15–16–19–23
Red-footed Falcon	Falco vespertinus	Cernícalo Patirrojo	Acc	9
Merlin	Falco columbarius	Esmerejón	M–W	9–17–19–23
Hobby	Falco subbuteo	Alcotán Europeo	b–m–w	2–4–13–23
Lanner Falcon	Falco biarmicus	Halcón Borní	Acc	9
Peregrine Falcon	Falco peregrinus	Halcón Peregrino	b–M–W	9–13–14–17–19
RALLIDAE				
Water Rail	Rallus aquaticus	Rascón Europeo	B–M–W	8–10–16–17–20
Spotted Crake	Porzana porzana	Polluela Pintoja	m	9–16–19–20
Little Crake	Porzana parva	Polluela Bastarda	m	9
Baillon's Crake	Porzana pusilla	Polluela Chica	m	9
Moorhen	Gallinula chloropus	Gallineta Común	B–M–W	3–6–10–14–15–17
Purple Swamp-hen	Porphyrio porphyrio	Calamón Común	B–M–W	4–8–9–10–15–18–19
Common Coot	Fulica atra	Focha Común	B–M–W	3–6–9–13–17–20
Red-knobbed Coot	Fulica cristata	Focha Moruna	b–m–w	6–8–9–14–20

ENGLISH NAME	LATIN NAME	SPANISH NAME	Status	ITINERARY
	GRUIDAE			
Common Crane	*Grus grus*	Grulla Común	M–W	8–9–15
	OTIDIDAE			
Little Bustard	*Tetrax tetrax*	Sisón Común	m–w	8
	HAEMATOPODIDAE			
Oystercatcher	*Haematopus ostralegus*	Ostrero Euroasiático	M–W	1–22
	RECURVIROSTRIDAE			
Black-winged Stilt	*Himantopus himantopus*	Cigüeñuela Común	B–M–W	6–7–8–16–19–20
Avocet	*Recurvirostra avosetta*	Avoceta Común	B–M–W	6–14–19–20–21
	BURHINIDAE			
Stone Curlew	*Burhinus oedicnemus*	Alcaraván Común	B–M–W	1–9–16–19–23
	GLAREOLIDAE			
Collared Pratincole	*Glareola pratincola*	Canastera Común	B–M	7–10–16–17–18
	CHARADRIIDAE			
Little Ringed Plover	*Charadrius dubius*	Chorlitejo Chico	B–M–W	7–10–14–15–17
Ringed Plover	*Charadrius hiaticula*	Chorlitejo Grande	M–W	7–8–13–17–18
Kentish Plover	*Charadrius alexandrinus*	Chorlitejo Patinegro	B–M–W	1–10–15–19–21–22
Dotterel	*Charadrius morinellus*	Chorlito Carambolo	m–w	9–23
European Golden Plover	*Pluvialis apricaria*	Chorlito Dorado Europeo	M–W	9–10–17–20–23
Grey Plover	*Pluvialis squatarola*	Chorlito Gris	M–W	20–22
Sociable Lapwing	*Vanellus gregarius*	Avefría Sociable	Acc	15
Northern Lapwing	*Vanellus vanellus*	Avefría Europea	b–M–W	6–15–17–20–23
	SCOLOPACIDAE			
Knot	*Calidris canutus*	Correlimos Gordo	M–W	1–21–22
Sanderling	*Calidris alba*	Correlimos Tridáctilo	M–W	1–21–22
Little Stint	*Calidris minuta*	Correlimos Menudo	M–W	7–10–14–15–19
Temminck's Stint	*Calidris temminckii*	Correlimos de Temminck	M–W	8–10–18–19
Pectoral Sandpiper	*Calidris melanotos*	Correlimos Pectoral	Acc	10
Curlew Sandpiper	*Calidris ferruginea*	Correlimos Zarapitín	M–W	1–7–14–21–22
Dunlin	*Calidris alpina*	Correlimos Común	M–W	6–7–10–15–19
Ruff	*Philomachus pugnax*	Combatiente	M–W	6–8–10–14–19
Jack Snipe	*Lymnocryptes minimus*	Agachadiza Chica	m–w	15–19
Common Snipe	*Gallinago gallinago*	Agachadiza Común	M–W	4–8–13–14–15–18
Long-billed Dowitcher	*Limnodromus scolopaceus*	Agujeta Escolopácea	Acc	6
Woodcock	*Scolopax rusticola*	Chocha Perdiz	m–w	2
Black-tailed Godwit	*Limosa limosa*	Aguja Colinegra	M–W	6–10–15–20–21
Bar-tailed Godwit	*Limosa lapponica*	Aguja Colipinta	M–W	1–21–22
Whimbrel	*Numenius phaeopus*	Zarapito Trinador	M–W	20--21–22

ENGLISH NAME	LATIN NAME	SPANISH NAME	Status	ITINERARY
Eurasian Curlew	Numenius arquata	Zarapito Real	M–W	15–20–21–22
Spotted Redshank	Tringa erythropus	Archibebe Oscuro	M–W	6–10–15–20–21
Common Redshank	Tringa totanus	Archibebe Común	B–M–W	7–14–18–20–21
Marsh Sandpiper	Tringa stagnatilis	Archibebe Fino	m–w	14–20
Greenshank	Tringa nebularia	Archibebe Claro	M–W	7–10–15–18–20
Greater Yellowlegs	Tringa melanoleuca	Archibebe Patigualdo Grande	Acc	9
Green Sandpiper	Tringa ochropus	Andarríos Grande	M–W	3–6–9–18–20
Wood Sandpiper	Tringa glareola	Andarríos Bastardo	M–W	6–8–9–18–19
Common Sandpiper	Actitis hypoleucos	Andarríos Chico	M–W	6–9–13–18–21
Turnstone	Arenaria interpres	Vuelvepiedras Común	M–W	21–22
Red-necked Phalarope	Phalaropus lobatus	Falaropo Picofino	m–w	21
	STERCORARIIDAE			
Arctic Skua	Stercorarius parasiticus	Págalo Parásito	M–W	1–22
Great Skua	Stercorarius skua	Págalo Grande	M–W	1–22
	LARIDAE			
Mediterranean Gull	Larus melanocephalus	Gaviota Cabecinegra	M–W	21–22
Little Gull	Larus minutus	Gaviota Enana	m–w	8–9
Black-headed Gull	Larus ridibundus	Gaviota Reidora	B–M–W	6–8–15–16–19
Slender-billed Gull	Larus genei	Gaviota Picofina	B–M–W	21–22
Audouin's Gull	Larus audouinii	Gaviota de Audouin	M–W	1–21–22
Ring-billed Gull	Larus delawarensis	Gaviota de Delaware	Acc	21
Lesser Black-backed Gull	Larus fuscus	Gaviota Sombría	M–W	8–10–15–18–19
Yellow-legged Gull	Larus michahellis	Gaviota Patiamarilla	B–M–W	1–20–21–22
Greater Black-backed Gull	Larus marinus	Gavión Atlántico	m–w	1–22
	STERNIDAE			
Gull-billed Tern	Sterna nilotica	Pagaza Piconegra	B–M	6–9–14–15–19
Caspian Tern	Sterna caspia	Pagaza Piquirroja	M–W	21–22
Royal Tern	Sterna maxima	Charrán Real	Acc	22
Lesser Crested Tern	Sterna bengalensis	Charrán Bengalí	m	22
Sandwich Tern	Sterna sandvicensis	Charrán Patinegro	M–W	1–21–22
Common Tern	Sterna hirundo	Charrán Común	M	1–21–22
Arctic Tern	Sterna paradisaea	Charrán Ártico	m	22
Little Tern	Sterna albifrons	Charrancito Común	B–M	19–21–22
Whiskered Tern	Chlidonias hybrida	Fumarel Cariblanco	B–M–w	6–8–9–17–19–20
Black Tern	Chlidonias niger	Fumarel Común	b–M	9–14–17–19–20
White-winged Black Tern	Chlidonias leucopterus	Fumarel Aliblanco	m	6–14–17
	ALCIDAE			
Common Guillemot	Uria aalge	Arao Común	m–w	1–22
Razorbill	Alca torda	Alca Común	m–w	1–22
Atlantic Puffin	Fratercula arctica	Frailecillo Atlántico	m–w	1–22

ENGLISH NAME	LATIN NAME	SPANISH NAME	Status	ITINERARY
	PTEROCLIDIDAE			
Pin-tailed Sandgrouse	*Pterocles alchata*	Ganga Ibérica	B–M–W	8–9–16–18–20–23
	COLUMBIDAE			
Stock Dove	*Columba oenas*	Paloma Zurita	m–w	5–11
Common Woodpigeon	*Columba palumbus*	Paloma Torcaz	B–M–W	2–5–11–12
Eurasian Collared Dove	*Streptopelia decaocto*	Tórtola Turca	B–M–W	4–11
European Turtle Dove	*Streptopelia turtur*	Tórtola Europea	B–M	2–7–12
	CUCULIDAE			
Great Spotted Cuckoo	*Clamator glandarius*	Críalo Europeo	B–M	2–14–19
Common Cuckoo	*Cuculus canorus*	Cuco Común	B–M	3–4–11–12
	TYTONIDAE			
Barn Owl	*Tyto alba*	Lechuza Común	B–M–W	7–10–12–18–20
	STRIGIDAE			
Scops Owl	*Otus scops*	Autillo Europeo	B–M	5–11
Eagle Owl	*Bubo bubo*	Búho Real	b–m–w	18
Little Owl	*Athene noctua*	Mochuelo Común	B–M–W	5–7–11–14–17
Tawny Owl	*Strix aluco*	Cárabo Europeo	B–M–W	4–5--11–12–21
Long-eared Owl	*Asio otus*	Búho Chico	B–M–W	2–12–21
Short-eared Owl	*Asio flammeus*	Búho Campestre	M–W	9–13–16–18–19
	CAPRIMULGIDAE			
European Nightjar	*Caprimulgus europaeus*	Chotacabras Gris	M	3–5
Red-necked Nightjar	*Caprimulgus ruficollis*	Chotacabras Pardo	B–M	2–7–11–12–18
	APODIDAE			
Alpine Swift	*Apus melba*	Vencejo Real	M	2–18–23
Common Swift	*Apus apus*	Vencejo Común	B–M	13–14–18–23
Pallid Swift	*Apus pallidus*	Vencejo Pálido	B–M	3–13–14–18–23
Little Swift	*Apus affinis*	Vencejo Moro	Acc	22
	ALCEDINIDAE			
Kingfisher	*Alcedo atthis*	Martín Pescador Común	M–W	3–6–16–17–21
	MEROPIDAE			
European Bee-eater	*Merops apiaster*	Abejaruco Europeo	B–M	7–8–11–13–14–17
	CORACIIDAE			
Roller	*Coracias garrulus*	Carraca Europea	M	13–18
	UPUPIDAE			
Hoopoe	*Upupa epops*	Abubilla	B–M–W	2–4–11–12–18–23
	PICIDAE			
Wryneck	*Jynx torquilla*	Torcecuello Euroasiático	M–w	4–11

ENGLISH NAME	LATIN NAME	SPANISH NAME	Status	ITINERARY
Green Woodpecker	Picus viridis	Pito Real	B–M–W	3–11–12–18
Great Spotted Woodpecker	Dendrocopos major	Pico Picapinos	B–M–W	2–5–11
	ALAUDIDAE			
Calandra Lark	Melanocorypha calandra	Calandria Común	B–M–W	7–8–18
Short-toed Lark	Calandrella brachydactyla	Terrera Común	B–M	8–9–16–18–19
Lesser Short-toed Lark	Calandrella rufescens	Terrera Marismeña	B–M–W	8–9–15–16–20–23
Crested Lark	Galerida cristata	Cogujada Común	B–M–W	7–8–15–16–17–23
Thekla Lark	Galerida theklae	Cogujada Montesina	B–M–W	2–5–12
Woodlark	Lullula arborea	Alondra Totovía	B–M–W	11–12–18
Skylark	Alauda arvensis	Alondra Común	M–W	8–9–10–13–17
	HIRUNDINIDAE			
Sand Martin	Riparia riparia	Avión Zapador	B–M–w	3–9–10–16–17
Barn Swallow	Hirundo rustica	Golondrina Común	B–M–w	3–5–6–13–17–23
Red-rumped Swallow	Hirundo daurica	Golondrina Dáurica	B–M	5–7–8–13–16
House Martin	Delichon urbicum	Avión Común	B–M–w	3–5–6–10–17
	MOTACILLIDAE			
Richard's Pipit	Anthus richardi	Bisbita de Richard	m–w	16
Tawny Pipit	Anthus campestris	Bisbita Campestre	M	8–9–23
Tree Pipit	Anthus trivialis	Bisbita Arbóreo	M	7–12–17
Meadow Pipit	Anthus pratensis	Bisbita Pratense	M–W	5–6–8–10–15–17
Water Pipit	Anthus spinoletta	Bisbita Alpino	M–W	9–19
Yellow Wagtail	Motacilla flava	Lavandera Boyera	B–M	7–10–16–17–20–23
Grey Wagtail	Motacilla cinerea	Lavandera Cascadeña	m–w	7–11
White Wagtail	Motacilla alba	Lavandera Blanca	M–W	6–8–10–17–18
	TROGLODYTIDAE			
Wren	Troglodytes troglodytes	Chochín Común	B–M–W	4–5–11
	PRUNELLIDAE			
Dunnock	Prunella modularis	Acentor Común	m–w	3–13
	TURDIDAE			
Rufous Bush Robin	Cercotrichas galactotes	Alzacola Rojizo	b–m	11–18
Robin	Erithacus rubecula	Petirrojo Europeo	M–W	2–5–12–14–18
Common Nightingale	Luscinia megarhynchos	Ruiseñor Común	B–M	3–5–7–11–13
Bluethroat	Luscinia svecica	Ruiseñor Pechiazul	M–W	6–9–15–16–18
Black Redstart	Phoenicurus ochruros	Colirrojo Tizón	M–W	1–5–6–12–17
Common Redstart	Phoenicurus phoenicurus	Colirrojo Real	M	5–9–17
Whinchat	Saxicola rubetra	Tarabilla Norteña	M	9–15–17
Common Stonechat	Saxicola torquatus	Tarabilla Común	B–M–W	2–4–5–15–18
Northern Wheatear	Oenanthe oenanthe	Collalba Gris	M	9–12–18–23
Black-eared Wheatear	Oenanthe hispanica	Collalba Rubia	b–M	2–3–18–23

ENGLISH NAME	LATIN NAME	SPANISH NAME	Status	ITINERARY
Ring Ouzel	*Turdus torquatus*	Mirlo Capiblanco	m	2
Blackbird	*Turdus merula*	Mirlo Común	B–M–W	3–4–5–12–18
Song Thrush	*Turdus philomelos*	Zorzal Común	M–W	4–5–11–12–14
Redwing	*Turdus iliacus*	Zorzal Alirrojo	M–W	5--11–13–14
Mistle Thrush	*Turdus viscivorus*	Zorzal Charlo	B–M–W	2–5–6
	SYLVIIDAE			
Cetti's Warbler	*Cettia cetti*	Ruiseñor Bastardo	B–M–W	5–6–13–15–17
Zitting Cisticola	*Cisticola juncidis*	Buitrón	B–M–W	7–10–13–19–20
Grasshopper Warbler	*Locustella naevia*	Buscarla Pintoja	M	4–5–17–20
Savi's Warbler	*Locustella luscinioides*	Buscarla Unicolor	B–M	3–10–15–18–19
Aquatic Warbler	*Acrocephalus paludicola*	Carricerín Cejudo	m	15
Sedge Warbler	*Acrocephalus schoenobaenus*	Carricerín Común	M	9–10–19
Reed Warbler	*Acrocephalus scirpaceus*	Carricero Común	B–M	3–10–15–17–19
Great Reed Warbler	*Acrocephalus arundinaceus*	Carricero Tordal	B–M	3–10–15–16–19
Western Olivaceous Warbler	*Hippolais opaca*	Zarcero Pálido Occidental	B–M	8–13–17–18
Melodious Warbler	*Hippolais polyglotta*	Zarcero Común	B–M	2–4–11–12
Dartford Warbler	*Sylvia undata*	Curruca Rabilarga	B–M–W	1–2–5–13
Spectacled Warbler	*Sylvia conspicillata*	Curruca Tomillera	B–M	4–5–12–20–23
Subalpine Warbler	*Sylvia cantillans*	Curruca Carrasqueña	M	2–12–18
Sardinian Warbler	*Sylvia melanocephala*	Curruca Cabecinegra	B–M–W	1–2–4–5–12–18
Western Orphean Warbler	*Sylvia hortensis*	Curruca Mirlona	M	5–11
Common Whitethroat	*Sylvia communis*	Curruca Zarcera	M	2–4–17
Garden Warbler	*Sylvia borin*	Curruca Mosquitera	M	2–4–18
Blackcap	*Sylvia atricapilla*	Curruca Capirotada	b–M–W	2–3–11–12–14
Bonelli's Warbler	*Phylloscopus bonelli*	Mosquitero Papialbo	M	2–5
Iberian Chiffchaff	*Phylloscopus ibericus*	Mosquitero Ibérico	M	5–13–21
Common Chiffchaff	*Phylloscopus collybita*	Mosquitero Común	M–W	2–5–13–15–21
Willow Warbler	*Phylloscopus trochilus*	Mosquitero Musical	M	2–5–13–21
Firecrest	*Regulus ignicapilla*	Reyezuelo Listado	M–W	2–5
	MUSCICAPIDAE			
Spotted Flycatcher	*Muscicapa striata*	Papamoscas Gris	B–M	2–4–5–17
Pied Flycatcher	*Ficedula hypoleuca*	Papamoscas Cerrojillo	M	4–5–17
	AEGITHALIDAE			
Long-tailed Tit	*Aegithalos caudatus*	Mito	B–M–W	2–3–4–5
	PARIDAE			
Crested Tit	*Parus cristatus*	Herrerillo Capuchino	B–M–W	5–11–12
Blue Tit	*Parus caeruleus*	Herrerillo Común	B–M–W	3–5–11–12
Great Tit	*Parus major*	Carbonero Común	B–M–W	2–5–11–12–18
	CERTHIIDAE			
Short-toed Treecreeper	*Certhia brachydactyla*	Agateador Común	B–M–W	2–4–5–11–12

ENGLISH NAME	LATIN NAME	SPANISH NAME	Status	ITINERARY
	REMIZIDAE			
Penduline Tit	*Remiz pendulinus*	Pájaro Moscón	B–M–W	4–10–11–13–18–19
	ORIOLIDAE			
Golden Oriole	*Oriolus oriolus*	Oropéndola	M	2–11–12–18
	LANIIDAE			
Southern Grey Shrike	*Lanius meridionalis*	Alcaudón Real	B–M–W	2–11–12–13
Woodchat Shrike	*Lanius senator*	Alcaudón Común	B–M	7–11–14–18–23
	CORVIDAE			
Azure-winged Magpie	*Cyanopica cyanus*	Rabilargo	B–M–W	1–3–5–11–12–21
Magpie	*Pica pica*	Urraca	B–M–W	1–3–4–8–15–21
Eurasian Jackdaw	*Corvus monedula*	Grajilla	B–M–W	10–14
Common Raven	*Corvus corax*	Cuervo	B–M–W	2–5–11–12–21
	STURNIDAE			
Common Starling	*Sturnus vulgaris*	Estornino Pinto	M–W	2–5–8–9–15–19
Spotless Starling	*Sturnus unicolor*	Estornino Negro	B–M–W	2–4–8–12–16–19
Rose-coloured Starling	*Sturnus roseus*	Estornino Rosado	Acc	19
	PASSERIDAE			
House Sparrow	*Passer domesticus*	Gorrión Común	B–M–W	3–12–14–15–17–19
Spanish Sparrow	*Passer hispaniolensis*	Gorrión Moruno	B–M–W	8–10–14–17–18–19
Tree Sparrow	*Passer montanus*	Gorrión Molinero	B–M–W	5–7–11–12–14–17
Rock Sparrow	*Petronia petronia*	Gorrión Chillón	b–M–W	11
	PLOCEIDAE			
Yellow-crowned Bishop	*Euplectes afer*	Tejedor Amarillo	B–M–W	10--19
	ESTRILDIDAE			
Common Waxbill	*Estrilda astrild*	Pico de Coral	B–M–W	11–17
Black-rumped Waxbill	*Estrilda troglodytes*	Estrilda Culinegro	B–M–W	10–17
Red Avadavat	*Amandava amandava*	Bengalí Rojo	b–m–w	17
	FRINGILLIDAE			
Common Chaffinch	*Fringilla coelebs*	Pinzón Vulgar	B–M–W	4–5–11–12–21
Brambling	*Fringilla montifringilla*	Pinzón Real	m–w	5
European Serin	*Serinus serinus*	Verdecillo	B–M–W	1–7–12–18
Greenfinch	*Carduelis chloris*	Verderón Común	B–M–W	1–7–13–18
Goldfinch	*Carduelis carduelis*	Jilguero	B–M–W	1–7–12–17
Siskin	*Carduelis spinus*	Lúgano	M–W	11–13
Linnet	*Carduelis cannabina*	Pardillo Común	B–M–W	1–9–16–19–23
Common Bullfinch	*Pyrrhula pyrrhula*	Camachuelo Común	M–W	5–11
Hawfinch	*Coccothraustes coccothraustes*	Picogordo	b–m–w	12
	EMBERIZIDAE			
Cirl Bunting	*Emberiza cirlus*	Escribano Soteño	B–M–W	5–7–11
Reed Bunting	*Emberiza schoeniclus*	Escribano Palustre	M–W	8–9–10–16–19
Corn Bunting	*Emberiza calandra*	Triguero	B–M–W	7–8–12–17–19–23

TABLE-SUMMARY OF ITINERARIES

ITINERARY

UTM START	UTM END	km by vehicle	km on foot	Habitat	Province
1. El Médano del Asperillo					
29S 705757	29S 0705757	0	4	Coast	Huelva
4106514	4106514				
2. El Abalario and Ribetehilos					
29S 702466	29S 707882	7.5	2.5	Pinewoods/	Huelva
4108508	4112489			Monte blanco	
3. El Acebuche and Sector 15					
29S 716499	29S 718221	2.1	2.8	Lagoons/	Huelva
4102913	4108437			Pastures	
4. El Arroyo de La Rocina					
29S 722503	29S 722503	0	3.5	Thicket/	Huelva
4111682	4111682			Stream	
5. El Charco del Acebrón					
29S 722503	29S 718105	5.4	1.5	Cork Oak/	Huelva
4111682	4113661			Thicket	
6. The marshes of El Rocío					
29S 723966	29S 722669	0	2	Marshland	Huelva
4112227	4111861				
7. El Arroyo del Partido (or Arroyo de la Palmosa)					
29S 725800	29S 725800	0	4.6	Stream/	Huelva
4117502	4117502			Agricultural	
8. La Dehesa de Pilas and El Caño del Guadiamar					
29S 748251	29S 732435	30.2	0	Pastures/	Seville
4118480	4106780			Marshland	
9. El Lucio del Lobo and El Muro de la FAO					
29S 748338	29S 729854	27.3	0	Agriculture/	Seville/
4115795	4110357			Marshland	Huelva
10. El Brazo de la Torre (northern sector)					
29S 750044	29S 749357	4.3	0.8	Rice-paddies/	Seville
4120684	4120254			Marshland	
11. El Arroyo del Algarbe and the Hinojos pinewoods					
29S 732700	29S 730614	22	0	Riparian	Huelva
4131452	4129391			woodland/	
				Pinewoods	

ITINERARY

UTM START	UTM END	km by vehicle	km on foot	Habitat	Province
12. The Aznalcázar pinewoods					
29S 745555	29S 0742960	12.6	2.6	Pinewoods/	Seville
4129090	4126281			Dehesa	
13. El Corredor Verde del Guadiamar (northern sector)					
29S 745514	29S 748251	20.1	0	Agricultural/	Seville
4129111	4118480			Lagoons	
14. La Dehesa de Abajo and La Cañada de Rianzuela					
29S 751348	29S 749035	12	2	Olive tree	Seville
4121348	4115021			woodland/	
				Lagoons	
15. Cantarita and El Brazo de la Torre (southern sector)					
29S 751266	29S 746410	15	0	Rice-paddies/	Seville
4112918	4102048			Marshland	
16. El Corredor Verde (southern sector). Entremuros del Guadiamar					
29S 751348	29S 742326	35	0	Marshland	Seville
4121348	4099999				
17. La Corta de los Olivillos					
29S 764964	29S 761868	16.5	0	Agricultural/	Seville
4125931	4122885			Lagoons	
18. El Brazo del Este I					
29S 764964	30S 233724	15.3	0	Marshland	Seville
4125931	4119157				
19. El Brazo del Este II					
29S 732700	30S 238623	16	0	Rice-paddies/	Seville
4131452	4116708			Marshland	
20. From Trebujena to the Monte Algaida saltpans					
29S 751427	29S 736885	17	0.7	Salt-marshes/	Cádiz
4084628	4084591			Saltpans	
21. The Bonanza saltpans and La Algaida pinewood					
29S 737667	29S 739460	4.5	0.5	Salt-marshes/	Cádiz
4078805	4081465			Pinewoods	
22. The beaches of Montijo and La Jara					
29S 731805	29S 731805	0	6	Coastal	Cádiz
4071673	4071673				
23. The marshes of Trebujena					
29S 744560	29S 743102	8.4	2.4	Salt-marshes	Cádiz
4075828	4073848				

Itinerary nº 1

EL MÉDANO DEL ASPERILLO

*La Playa de Castilla
and Cuesta Maneli*

> **BASIC INFORMATION**
>
> **Start and end:** Car-park at Cuesta Maneli (29S 705757 4106514)
> **Distance:** around 4 km on foot
> **Map:** SGE 10-42 (scale 1:50,000)
> **Municipalities:** Almonte (Huelva)

Facing the Atlantic Ocean to the west of Matalascañas lies El Médano de Asperillo, one of the most fascinating geological monuments on the Andalusian coastline. El Médano represents the leading edge of a dune cordon that was once advancing inland. A period of uplift led to the formation of the cliff – or *médano* – that today runs for a number of kilometres between Matalascañas and Arroyo del Loro (also known as the Playa de Castilla). The semi-stable dune cordon was fixed by planting umbrella pines, although today there are still two small fronts of activity about 600 m to the east where you can see piles of fallen pine trunks (*cruces*) half-swallowed up by the advancing sand.

At 106 m above sea-level, this is the highest point in the whole area and a boardwalk (around 1,200 m) known as Cuesta Maneli runs the whole length of this beautiful and singular site.

Our first itinerary brings you into contact with the seabirds and other birds of the sandy beaches; as well, visitors will enjoy the wonderful views of the Atlantic and the flat expanses of El Abalario, a vast pine-covered plain that is bathed in golden light at sunset.

DESCRIPTION

You begin the route in the public car-park at km 39.5 of the A-494 (San Juan del Puerto-Matalascañas). Walk up the

El Médano del Asperillo and La Playa de Castilla   © Jorge Garzón

wooden boardwalk over the dunes to the highest part of the dune cordon.

Here you are surrounded by the white sands and the green of the pines, as well as all the typical shrubs of the *monte negro*: green heather (*Erica scoparia*), sage-leaved cistus (*Cistus salviifolius*) and *Rhamnus lycioides*. From the boardwalk you will hear the harsh calls of the Magpie, while families of Azure-winged Magpies move around the pines. In the lowest branches of the pines Black Redstarts await their prey, while finches such as Serin and Goldfinch search the ground for seeds.

The itinerary is equipped with information panels that help to interpret the flora and the landscape, as well as the tracks left by reptiles and mammals in the sand. You won't fail to miss the abundant *Corema album*, a curious heather-like shrub that is classified as 'vulnerable' by the Red Data Book of the Flora of Andalusia. The fruit of this plant consists of white-coloured balls, full of water and glucose, that are the main source of water for birds and mammals alike during the dry season. The best time to look for two of Doñana's most restless birds – Sardinian and Dartford Warblers – is as they search for insects and water when the fruit of *Corema album* are ripe.

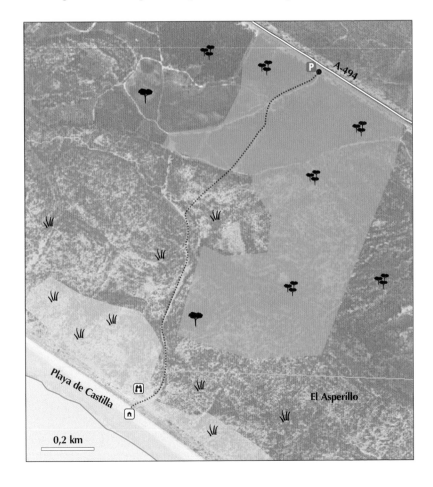

Stone Curlew © José Antonio Sencianes

As you approach the sea the pines begin to assume low twisted forms as they lean away from the *foreño*, the prevailing wind that blows from the west. Soon the horizon opens and the full extent of the sea becomes apparent as you reach the natural step down to Playa de Castilla at the edge of the *médano* of fossilised sand. This is an excellent place for seawatching in winter and during migration periods.

The first birds that become apparent against the blue background are Cory's Shearwaters, with their characteristic undulating passage over the waves, and Balearic Shearwaters, identifiable by their low straight flight. Somewhat higher fly the Northern Gannets who plunge arrow-like straight into sea in search of fish. Other species to be seen here in winter include the black silhouettes of Common Scoters riding the waves.

Further out your powers of observation are put to test. After a storm, migration steps up again and interesting observations of a number of auks can be made: Common Guillemots, Razorbills and even a few Atlantic Puffins with whirring wings all come quite close inshore.

One of the most memorable birdwatching sights is the persecution of one bird by another. From this raised vantage point it is easy to detect the light buoyant flight of the Sandwich Tern, often chased by Yellow-legged Gulls when they spot a tern with a fish in its beak. However, if the bird doing the chasing is dark all over, then the tern must fear for its life rather than the mere loss of its prey: we can vividly recall seeing both Great Skuas hunt down Common Terns and Arctic Skuas stoop on small gulls and terns and force them down into the water.

Leaving your viewpoint, drop down some wooden steps to the beautiful beach of Playa de Castilla, one the longest virgin beaches in the whole of

A group of Audouin's Gulls   © Francisco Chiclana

Spain. At low tide the vastness of the beach and the spectacular *médano* join and fade together into the distant haze. With your back to the sea you will notice that the vegetation only covers the sands in patches, the only really verdant areas being the small scattered depressions reaching the line of the beach where water upwells. Birds, reptiles and mammals come to drink here and it is not hard to locate these small oases by following the fluttering flight of Linnets and Greenfinches searching for water.

At the water's edge you will see groups of small birds running nervously to and fro. These are Sanderling and are accompanied by other waders such

PRACTICAL GUIDE

Other access points: You can reach the starting point of the itinerary along the A-494 (San Juan del Puerto-Matalascañas) from Mazagón and Huelva.

Additional information: Aside from the protection afforded by the Doñana National Park, El Médano del Asperillo is legally protected as a Natural Monument. There is no information centre; in summer a rubbish collection service cleans the beach and there is a small bar.

Transport: A bus runs from Almonte and Matalascañas to Mazagón and Huelva (and vice versa) via Cuesta Maneli, although you must ask the driver to stop. During the summer the car-park is superintended and you have to pay. The nearest petrol station is three kilometres from Matalascañas on the A-483 (closed at night).

Water and toilets: In summer there is a small bar/restaurant on the beach. During the rest of the year you must rely on the bars and restaurants in Matalascañas. The small springs in the small depressions are not easily accessible.

Wheelchair access: The boardwalk is flat and stable and rotten boards are replaced. However, there is no wheelchair access to the beach.

Recommendation: Groups of gulls are easily observed just after sunrise and so the best time to visit is the morning. Nevertheless, the light is better in the afternoon when you have better chances of seeing pelagic bird species. Whatever, avoid midday and use a telescope for seawatching.

as Curlew Sandpiper or the rather scarcer Knot. Feeding amongst the foam of the breaking waves you'll see Oystercatchers, with their long red bills and contrasting black and white plumage, as well as Bar-tailed Godwits digging energetically in the temporary pools formed by the waves. Groups of gulls hang around the beach itself and here you should look for Audouin's and Greater Black-backed Gulls, the latter noticeably larger than the other gulls. Here and there the delicate and watchful Kentish Plovers run around on the sands.

Return to the car-park by the same route without forgetting to cast another gaze over the sea from the cliff top in search of two of the most beautiful but scarce birds in Doñana, Red-throated and Great Northern Divers, both of which winter here in small numbers. If your return to the car-park is at dusk, you'll be sure to hear the call of the Stone Curlew.

Itinerary nº 2

EL ABALARIO AND RIBETEHILOS

La Vereda del Loro and El Monte de Cabezudos

BASIC INFORMATION

Start: km 35.7 of A-494 (29S 702466 4108508)
End: Beginning of Ribetehilos path (29S 707882 4112489)
Distance: 7.5 km by vehicle and 2.5 km on foot
Map: SGE 10-42 (scale 1:50,000)
Municipalities: Almonte (Huelva)

The great plain stretching northwards from the road from Matalascañas to Mazagón is known as El Monte de Abalario and Cabezudos and consists of a vast sandy extension of fixed dunes that since the 1940s and 1950s has been disfigured by many pine and eucalyptus plantations.

The boardwalk at Ribetehilos © Jorge Garzón

Here too you will find Ribetehilos, a name that is a corruption of the phrase *hilera de riberas*, that is, 'line of riversides'. This name refers to the exuberant vegetation – strawberry trees, myrtles, *Phillyrea angustifolia* and riverside trees, as well as a number of endemic plants in the peat bogs – that occurs here on and around a line of springs that seep out in the contact zone between two layers of sands.

It is an ideal place for birdwatching during migration periods because the numerous small birds that gather here also attract birds of prey. Try and come at dusk, when the peace and quiet of the area and the changing light allow you to forget the hurly-burly of everyday life.

DESCRIPTION

The itinerary begins at km 35.7 of the A-494 (San Juan del Puerto-Matalascañas), where this road is joined by Vereda del Camino del Loro, a drover's road. A sign with a map easily identifies the spot; on the other side of the road another sign marks 'Camino Verde a Mazagón'. Resetting the kilometre marker of your car to zero, head north along a track into the rolling sandy wastes and stands of umbrella pines. On the electric wire to your left it is not uncommon to see Ravens or a Common Kestrel.

Every now and again broad bare firebreaks cross the track and it is worth looking here for mammals; despite being largely nocturnal, you might chance upon a Red Fox or an Egyptian Mongoose. Birdwise, look for Thekla Larks and Hoopoes in the bare areas. With practice, the former can be distinguished from the very similar Crested Lark by the ascending note at the end of its call.

Stopping wherever you want, after 4 km you pass next to a tall fire watchtower and a radio antenna and then just 100 m further on you come to a T-junction. You are now in El Monte del Abalario and from this slightly raised position, it's worth scanning the skies for Booted Eagles, Red Kite, or if you are lucky, a juvenile Spanish Imperial Eagle (called *pajizos* or 'straw-coloured' locally).

Turn right into an area of scrub with abundant Red-legged Partridge and Dartford Warbler, prey for the Hobbies

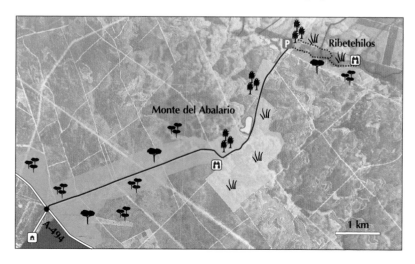

Booted Eagle © José Manuel Reyes

that hunt passerines and swifts in the area. Check out the tallest parts of the scrub for the unmistakeable silhouette of a Red or Fallow Deer. After 4.9 km you reach an open area with a picturesque lagoon (if it has rained) and the dismantled Poblado Forestal del Abalario. This settlement was built during the twentieth century during work on the plantations and even as late as 2003 charcoal-burners – the last in Doñana – were still working here transforming their smoking *boliches* (piles of wood) into charcoal for burning at home.

Next to the track a sign indicates 'Los Cabezudos', 'Los Bodegones' and 'Sendero de Ribetehilos'. Continue straight on along the track towards Ribetehilos, looking out for Black-eared Wheatears with their characteristic tail-wagging and whole families of Common Stonechat sitting atop the surrounding bushes. This is also a good spot to hear the peculiarly repetitive song of the Red-necked Nightjar.

The track becomes more sandy – but still easily driveable – from here on and after 7.5 km you reach the public car-park at Ribetehilos, right next to an eucalyptus plantation that stands out from the surrounding plains.

Being sure to park in the shade of a pine, start to walk along the wooden boardwalk that will take you deep into this remote part of Doñana. In autumn, keep an eye on the sky for migrating Alpine Swifts and European Turtle Doves, and in winter for groups of duck moving between the river Odiel and the flooded salt-marshes.

When their fruit are ripe, search in the tall strawberry-trees for insectivore birds such as Melodious and Garden Warblers and Common Whitethroat; in the wild olives and *Phillyrea* look out for the shy Golden Orioles, most easily detected by their harsh call.

A little further on the horizon clears and small cork oaks and stands of pines appear, home to the Great Spotted Woodpecker. Ideally you will be able to tune your hearing into the contact calls between migrating birds and in this way you might come across the scarce

Great Spotted Cuckoo   © Jorge Garzón

Ring Ouzel resting on its way to Africa. Other birds include Short-toed Treecreeper, the nervous Bonelli's Warbler, Spotted Flycatcher and Firecrest, the latter immediately identified by its high-pitched call.

Halfway along the path after passing through an area of peat bogs, you reach a junction: keep right alongside a stream choked with a line of dense vegetation. In the shade of a dense pinewood at the end of the path look under the trees for

PRACTICAL GUIDE

Other access points: You can reach the starting point of the itinerary along the A-494 (San Juan del Puerto-Matalascañas) from Mazagón and Huelva. From Almonte along HF-6248 passing through interesting scenery you can reach Los Cabezudos and from this settlement you can take the H-9016 forest track that leads to Ribetehilos and Abalario (only apt for 4WD vehicles).

Additional information: El Abalario and Ribetehilos lie within the Doñana National Park and since 1989 the Park authorities have been working to eliminate the eucalyptus plantations and restore the original vegetation. There is no information centre, although a series of panels provide information about the local vegetation and geology.

Transport: A bus runs from Almonte and Matalascañas to Mazagón and Huelva (and vice versa), although there is no official bus-stop at the start of the itinerary. Before you get on the bus you should ask the driver to stop 'non-officially'. The nearest petrol station is just outside the town of Mazagón.

Water and toilets: There are no toilets and you should also carry water.

Wheelchair access: Many interesting observations can be made from a vehicle and wheelchair users will find the track firm and stable, if somewhat sandy. The boardwalk is well looked after and rotten boards are replaced.

Recommendation: For those in 4WD vehicles, we recommend you continue onwards to El Monte de los Cabezudos along forest track H-9016, which will take you from Ribetehilos to the Poblado Forestal de los Cabezudos. In this way you can visit Arroyo de la Rocina next to Puente de las Ortigas. Return via the attractive HF-6248 to Mazagón or Almonte.

Few people frequent this area and so care must be taken on the sandy tracks if you are not in a 4WD vehicle.

Long-eared Owl pellets, while in the canopy Long-tailed and Great Tits, Willow Warblers, Chiffchaffs, Blackcaps and Robins add a touch of colour to the green of the foliage. Here too you may surprise a Red-legged Partridge. Return to the previous junction and turn right (the left turn from before) along a boardwalk over a marshy area.

A lot of rain is needed to fill the Laguna del Galápago and so probably you will be faced here with a dry extension of *monte negro* and a few taller shrubs. This is, however, a good spot for Sardinian and Subalpine Warblers and the boardwalk also provides excellent views of Southern Grey Shrike and groups of Great Spotted Cuckoos. Listen out for the repetitive song of the Song Thrush and the deep purring of the Wood Pigeon. Sparrowhawks perch on the solitary cork oaks and use this area as a hunting site during their migrations.

Continuing along the path you pass behind the stands of eucalyptus, where Common and Spotless Starling sing at sunset in winter, and return to the carpark.

Itinerary nº 3

EL ACEBUCHE AND SECTOR 15

Lagunas del Acebuche, El Huerto, Las Pajas and Finca del Alamillo

BASIC INFORMATION
Start: A-483, km 37.8 (29S 716499 4102913)
End: Fence of Sector 15 (29S 718221 4108437)
Distance: 2.1 km by vehicle and 2.8 km on foot.
Map: SGE 10-42 (scale 1:50,000)
Municipalities: (Almonte, Huelva)

Many of the visitors who come to Doñana head for the Acebuche Visitor Centre, the most important of all the information centres in the National Park. The Centre is housed in a sumptuous building, designed much in the style of the traditional farms of this part of Andalusia, and lies next to a series of lagoons with water almost all-year round. Here you will find all the typical birds of these habitats.

Laguna del Acebuche   © Jorge Garzón

The plains of El Alamillo   © Jorge Garzón

Here we describe just one of the possible routes in El Acebuche and leave it up to the reader to explore the western part of this interesting site. We also visit an all but unknown part of Doñana bordering on the Guayules Estate that is one of the few areas of steppe and dry marsh in the western part of the region, outside the National Park. These lands were once part of the Cortijo El Alamillo, an estate best known as Sector 15 in reference to the name given to it by the Plan Almonte-Marismas. However, this particular part is one of the few sectors included in the Plan that was not given over to intensive irrigated agriculture. This Plan, first implemented in 1971 and declared of national interest, aimed to use underground water supplies to irrigate 25,000 ha of sandy soils and marshes lying in the north-east of the National Park. Although it was never fully implemented, it did still destroy – in the full knowledge of the local administration – many very ecologically valuable areas of Doñana.

DESCRIPTION

The easy-to-find entrance to the Acebuche Visitor Centre is at km 37.8 of the A-483 (Bollullos Par del Condado-Matalascañas). The driveway in 1.5 km takes you to the car-park in front of the building. On getting out of your vehicle, three things will strike you straight away: firstly, the noise of the starlings, secondly, the enormous White Stork's nest on the top of the tower with its attendant House Sparrows, and thirdly the Azure-winged Magpies, here extraordinarily abundant in and amongst the picnic tables.

Head for the beginning of the trail behind the Centre, where you will immediately find signs for the different marked itineraries: to the left, Lagunas del Huerto y Las Pajas, and to the right Laguna del Acebuche. Turn right and after a short walk you will reach the first hide (Somormujo) and **Stop A**. From here there are good views of those water birds that need open water with well-vegetated banks: Little Grebe, Red-crested Pochard, Moorhen and Common Coot. From the pines in

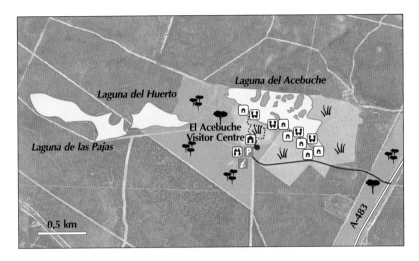

the background come the incessant calls of the Common Cuckoo in spring.

Continuing along the well-made boardwalk, check the white poplars and the white willows for passerines such as Blackbird, Long-tailed and Blue Tits and Blackcap. Soon you reach a semi-circular north-facing viewpoint with an information panel, a good spot for watching for circling raptors. A little further on you reach a second hide (Calamón) framed by enormous white poplars and home to feeding Dunnocks in winter. **Stop B** is inside this hide, from where there are good views over a large lagoon. Look out for Eurasian Wigeon, Gadwall, Common Teal and Pintail, as well as Purple Herons standing stock-still in the reeds. Listen out too for the laughing call of the Green Woodpecker, in Spain not the nominal subspecies, but subspecies *sharpei*.

Continue along the boardwalk into a drier scrubby area as far as a covered meeting point opposite another hide. The open area off to the right is used as a resting site by many migrants such as the low-flying Pallid Swift or – with luck – the European Nightjar, stopping off here on its long southward journey.

The third hide (Malvasía) with its two characteristic juniper trees is **Stop C**.

Azure-winged Magpie   © Diego López

Gadwall   © Mario Martín

Here the lagoon changes and patches of open water alternate with small, well-vegetated islands, ideal for the rare Ferruginous Duck and Little Bittern. This area is also favoured by Sand Martins for feeding, while Reed Warblers sing from the reedbeds. A metallic flash of blue signals the arrival of a Kingfisher on its way to fish from a prominent perch.

Two more hides remain and from either it is possible to hear the territorial songs of Great Reed and Savi's Warblers, the former powerful and strident, the latter a hard-to-locate whirring.

Return to the beginning of the itinerary and turn right and walk parallel to the bank of the lagoon as far as the last hide on this itinerary. Here the belt of vegetation around the lagoon is especially dense and the trees are good refuge for Common Nightingales, singing their explosive songs from the heart of the thicket. Barn Swallows hunt insects among the neighbouring wild olive and pines. Soon you reach the last stop (**Stop D**) in the final hide (Zampullín), from where broad views open out new panoramas over the lagoon. Look for three species if you haven't seen them already: Great Crested Grebe with its spectacular courtship, European Pochard and occasional hybrids between this species and other diving ducks, and the unmistakeable silhouette of Northern Shoveler, here in one of its favourite sites. Return from here to the car-park

Leave the Visitor Centre and return to the road. Turn towards El Rocío and continue along the A-483 north-east for 6 km. Exactly at km 31.9, turn left (it is best to pull off the road to the right before crossing) along a small badly paved road with a narrow canal running along the right-hand side. You are now entering Sector 17, whose marshes were not as lucky as those of Sector 15 and were transformed by the Plan Almonte-Marismas into the greenhouse cultivation you can see today.

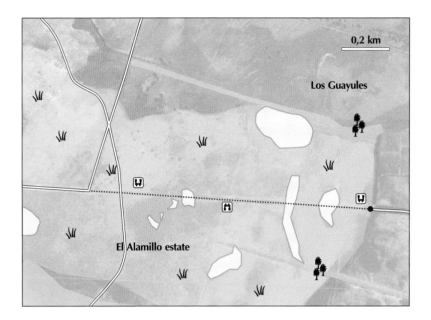

Continue straight on for 2.5 km along this road lined with exotic trees such as Australian acacias and common thorn-apples and into a large estate whose entrance is marked by a sign 'Finca adscrita por la CAM al Plan de Aprovechamiento Ganadero del Parque Nacional de Doñana'. Reset your kilometre counter to zero and enter Sector 15. There are no exact stopping

PRACTICAL GUIDE

Other access points: You can reach the starting point of the itinerary along the A-483 (Bollullos Par del Condado-Matalascañas) from Matalascañas and Mazagón.

Additional information: The Acebuche Visitor Centre is the most important public infrastructure in the National Park. Check the opening times before you visit: normally it is open from 08.00 to 21.00 in summer and 09.00 to 19.00 in winter. The lagoons of El Acebuche, El Huerto and Las Pajas are part of the Park's Special Protection Zone. All are known generically as *Las Lagunas de Los Pájaros*.

The publicly owned Alamillo estate – where cows are taken to relieve grazing pressure on the National Park – can be entered freely as long as you do not leave the road.

Transport: A bus runs from Almonte to Matalascañas (and vice versa). There is a stop at the entrance to El Acebuche and to the road to El Alamillo (ask the driver to drop you at *La Pequeña Holanda*).

Water and toilets: The Visitor Centre has toilets, restaurant and cafeteria.

Wheelchair access: There are no obstacles for wheelchair users; the boardwalk is well looked after and rotten boards are replaced.

Recommendation: Avoid midday in summer and wear insect repellent. These lagoons dry up in summer and so some of the birds mentioned may be absent. Walk in silence in order to be able to detect small passerines, whose presence is often only revealed by their calls.

points and the return is along the same road, in total 4.2 km there and back.

Like the other marshes in Doñana, this area changes completely from the wet to the dry season. If the rains are abundant this marsh will flood for three months and then resting and feeding waders are common. Groups of Green Sandpipers are amongst the commonest birds; note too the nine electric pylons that cross Sector 15, each with its own White Stork nest. Magpies come out to greet you as you pass through the gate.

The most interesting birds of these rich pastures are those that frequent these semi-steppe areas. Look for Black-eared Wheatear and Red-legged Partridge, and if you are here in late afternoon you are almost guaranteed the sight of a Black-shouldered Kite hunting rodents over the pastures. After the breeding season is finished, whole families of hirundines gather here, the commonest species being the House Martin, which can be seen all-year round since there is a small but stable wintering population in Doñana.

Itinerary nº 4

EL ARROYO DE LA ROCINA
Charcos del Perchel and La Boca, Algaidas del Carrizal and Del Meloncillo

BASIC INFORMATION

Start and End: Public car-park at La Casa de la Rocina (29S 722503 4111682)
Distance: 3.5 km on foot
Map: SGE 11-42 (scale 1:50,000)
Municipalities: Almonte (Huelva)

El Arroyo de la Rocina is one of only two permanent sources of fresh water in the National Park. The final 12 km of this stream are included in the protected area and are thus safeguarded as perfect example of the *vera*, the habitat that consists of the contact zone between the marshes and the sandy flats covered by stands of pine and oak. In the area of La Rocina before it flows into the marshes at Puente de la Canariega there is a confluence of a number of exceptionally

The path crosses La Algaida del Carrizal   © Jorge Garzón

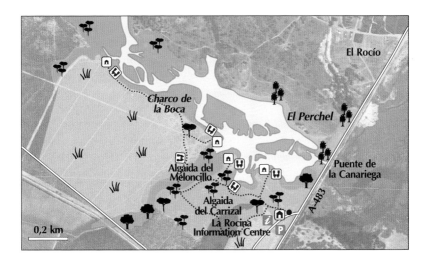

interesting habitats: fresh-water wetland, dense vegetation fringing the permanent lagoons, thickets, Mediterranean scrub and pine and deciduous woodland. Nevertheless, despite being protected, the *arroyo* is beginning to silt up and loose it water quality as a result of the illegal ploughing up of natural vegetation and the abusive use of fertilisers along the upper course of the stream.

La Rocina is one of the few places in Doñana where the public infrastructure is up to scratch and appropriate for naturalist searching for birds, flowers and even insects. Such facilities are much needed elsewhere in the park and as a rule the park authorities have failed to transmit to local people the natural values of Doñana, although obviously with naturalists this task as been much easier and more successful.

DESCRIPTION

The itinerary begins in the public carpark of La Rocina, which can be reached along the A-483 (Bollullos Par del Condado-Matalascañas) from the village of El Rocío. Just 100 m after

Heather fences in La Rocina © Jorge Garzón

passing over Puente de la Canariega turn right at the sign indicating 'Centro de Información de La Rocina'. Park in the free car-park and head first for a quick visit to the information centre that will provide you with a better idea of what birds you are likely to see.

Start this delightful itinerary by following the footpath towards Charco del Perchel, the name given to the final part of La Rocina. The path passes along the southern shore of the stream, here broad and with lushly vegetated banks.

At first you walk through a stand of umbrella pines where you will hear typical forest species such as Common Chaffinch, Long-tailed Tit, Blackbird, Magpie, Eurasian Collared Dove, Spotless Starling and Song Thrush. In a little while you will reach the first hide (La Espátula), a perfect spot for seeing Penduline Tit and Red-crested Pochard.

From here the itinerary reaches a first boardwalk that crosses a tributary of La Rocina known as La Algaida del Carrizal; listen out amongst the willows and ashes for Grasshopper Warblers, on the open water look for Common Teal and Garganey, and at the edge of the reed-beds look for Purple Swamp-hens extracting the pulp – their main food – from the inside of reed stems. In 2000 we saw here on a number of occasions a large raptor that we weren't at first able to identify. However, it turned out eventually to be one of a number of juvenile Spotted Eagles that appeared in Doñana that year and today juveniles of this species regularly winter here.

As we leave La Algaida and its bird song we return to the pines and reach a second hide (El Paraguas), where Wrens breed in the surrounding fence. The panorama from this hide is different and numerous water birds such as Common Snipe, Common Pochard, Northern Shoveler, Mallard, Gadwall and Glossy Ibis may parade in front of you. Listen out too for the sharp call of the Common Stonechat and look for Booted Eagle hunting in the skies.

On leaving this hide you will be surprised by the dense vegetation of this stretch of riparian woodland and will hear the characteristic calls of Pied and Spotted Flycatchers, whilst once in the pine woods, with an undergrowth of wild olive, lentisc and European fan-

Red-crested Pochard   © Jorge Garzón

Common Teal   © Mario Martín

PRACTICAL GUIDE

Other access points: You can reach the starting point of the itinerary along the A-483 (Bollullos Par del Condado-Matalascañas) from Matalascañas and Mazagón. Coming from Matalascañas the left turn is dangerous and we advise you to continue on to El Rocío and turn around there.

Additional information: The Arroyo de la Rocina is within the National Park's Special Protection Area and has an Information Office with a permanent exhibition on the wildlife of the area. Check the opening times before you visit: normally it is open from 09.00 to 19.00 in summer and 09.00 to 18.00 in winter. Opposite the centre there is a traditional hut with an interior that recreates the traditional lifestyle of the area and aspects of the mass annual pilgrimage to El Rocío. There are public toilets in the information centre.

Transport: A bus runs from Almonte and Matalascañas to El Rocío. From here it is easy to reach La Rocina on foot along the broad sandy track alongside the A-483 (which you then have to cross).

Water and toilets: In El Rocío the Casa de la Rocina has toilets and drinking water.

Wheelchair access: Access is generally fine and there are no special problems in getting into the hides. After rain the boardwalks can get rather slippery, especially when crossing the more humid streams.

Recommendation: Birds are less active at midday, although in winter any hour of the day is good for birdwatching. A telescope is necessary for the hides and binoculars for finding small birds in the reeds. This itinerary can be combined with nº 5 'El Charco del Acebrón' and nº 6 'The marshes of El Rocío'.

palm, the unmistakeable calls of Hoopoe and Common Cuckoo will accompany you.

You have to cross La Rocina again, this time passing through La Algaida del Meloncillo, and then reach a junction, where you should turn right. To a background of singing Melodious Warblers, enjoy this beautiful spot with its ferns – green in spring and ochre in autumn – and the white of *Halimium halimifolium*, the main component of the *monte blanco*. This is an ideal site for observing Sardinian, Spectacled and Garden Warblers and Common Whitethroat, whilst back in the pines you might surprise an alert Wryneck. This is also part of the hunting territory of the pair of Black-shouldered Kites that breed in the vicinity.

The third hide (Cuchara) looks out over El Charco de la Boca, the deepest part of the stream. Here it is easy to see Common Stonchats, Black Redstarts and various birds such as Reed and Great Reed Warblers moving in and out of the bulrushes. The muddy banks attract numerous species of waders.

Various species of hereon frequent this area and from the fourth hide (Cerceta carretona) there are excellent views of the heron roost that forms at dusk in the cork oaks and the trees that line La Rocina. Also at this time of day, the calls of the starlings fill the evening air and the Hobby makes its last forays of the day. The hooting of the Tawny Owl from the woods announces that night has fallen.

Return along the same path and hides, or alternatively continue straight on at the junction just after Algaida del Meloncillo and thence straight back to the car-park through woods with Short-toed Treecreeper, Common Cuckoos and numerous tits.

Itinerary nº 5

EL CHARCO DEL ACEBRÓN

BASIC INFORMATION
Start: Public car-park at La Rocina (29S 722503 4111682)
End: Public car-park at El Acebrón (29S 718105 4113661)
Distance: 5.4 km by vehicle and 1.5 km on foot
Maps: SGE 10-42 and 11-42 (1:50,000)
Municipalities: Almonte (Huelva)

El Acebrón is one our favourites spots in Doñana: it's an excellent place for all types of woodland birds and is, moreover, blessed by especially rich vegetation – magnificently intertwined lianas twist around the limbs of ancient cork

Entrance to El Palacio del Acebrón
© Jorge Garzón

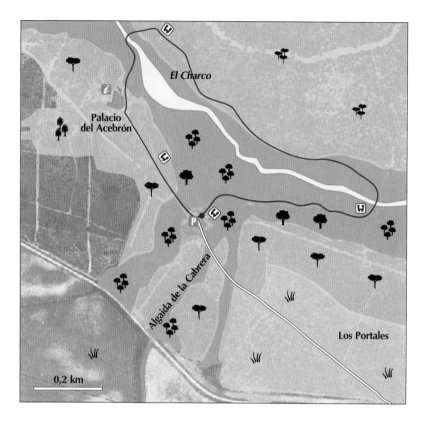

El Charco

Palacio del Acebrón

Algaida de la Cabrera

Los Portales

0,2 km

oaks – giving much needed shade on hot days. As well, the magnificent architecture of the palace and the silence that reigns in this site – unfortunately unlike much of the Park and its surroundings – is an added bonus.

El Palacio del Acebrón was built in 1961 by Luis Espinosa Fondevilla and in its day was a meeting place for rich hunters. Today it acts as one of the Park's visitor centres and is part of El Arroyo de la Rocina Special Protection Area.

DESCRIPTION

Begin the itinerary in the Arroyo de la Rocina public car-park (see itinerary nº 4) where, after resetting your kilometre counter to zero, you should head for the Acebrón Visitor Centre. Do not leave the made-up road as you are now within the National Park and in one of the hunting areas of the Pardel Lynx (*Lynx pardina*).

You will pass through an area of *monte blanco* (so-called because, unlike the *monte negro* found in other areas, there is here a predominance of the white-flowered *Halimium halimifolium*) and after 600 m, you will cross La Algaida del Carrizal: listen out here for the Common and Iberian Chiffchaffs and Willow and Grasshopper Warblers. From here on you will cross a number of other *algaidas* (the thickets that follow the water courses – the second comes just 1 km after the beginning of the itinerary) where you should stop to look and listen for birds up in the dense tree canopy.

After crossing the second *algaida*, you enter once again another large

Old cork oak   © Jorge Garzón

area of *monte blanco*, which is good for species such as Sardinian, Dartford and Spectacled Warblers and Thekla Lark, a lark that in general in Doñana lacks the large areas of untransformed open land it needs. In the background a line of trees reveals the presence of a stream – Arroyo de la Rocina – and provides refuge for Wood Pigeons and in winter the scarce Stock Dove. Common Stonechats will accompany you all the way through this section of the itinerary.

At 2 km from the start you will reach an area of spiny scrub known as Tojal del Berraco and then 1,100 m further on you will cross the third *algaida*, Algaida de Bernabé, characterised by a number of ancient cork oaks and numerous poplars. The canopy and branches are home to Common Chaffinch, Long-tailed Tit, Tree Sparrow, Western Orphean Warbler, Spotless Starling and thrushes such as Blackbird, Redwing and Mistle and Song Thrushes. In cold winters with invasions of birds from the north this is one of the few places in Doñana in which you might come across the rare Brambling.

The last *algaida* – Algaida de la Cabrera – comes just 100 m before the carpark, where you should park (5.4 km) and continue on foot.

From the right-hand side of the carpark and to the left of a huge cork oak, pick up one of the most beautiful of all the footpaths in the area. This path makes a circuit of the Charco del Acebrón and takes you through a number of different types of woodland.

It is best to walk in silence, stopping wherever necessary to study the birds. Be prepared to move your binoculars

Sardinian Warbler   © José Manuel Reyes

quickly as the birds move tirelessly through the canopy and keep you ears well open for songs and calls that will help you identify many of the species.

Common Stonechat   © Diego López

The most abundant birds here will be Great, Blue and, less commonly, Crested Tits, Common Bullfinch, Common Nightingale, Cetti's Warbler, Firecrest and Short-toed Treecreeper, amongst others, while overhead keep your eyes pealed for Azure-winged Magpie and Raven.

The first part of the path takes you into a singular peat-bog with relict plant species such as Dorset heath *Erica ciliaris* and the rare marsh gentian *Gentiana pneumonanthe*. The ground is densely covered by ferns (much-loved by the Wren), while between the cork oaks and the riparian woodland you may well surprise a Sparrowhawk or a Northern Goshawk wherever the tree cover is densest.

Soon you will enter into a patchwork of shade and light under the cover of mature cork oaks and wild olives, the remains of the forest that once covered the *vera* – the transition zone between marshland and pinewoods – in Doñana before the arrival of man. This is the domain of the Robin, easily detected by its short sharp call.

After crossing this thick patch of gallery forest, a large pinewood opens out in front of you, while to your left an impenetrable thickness of brambles, wild vines and other lianas provides shelter for numerous animal species.

Listen out for the call of the Great Spotted Woodpecker in the area between the pines and the stream; this is also a good spot for Bonelli's Warbler during migration and for both Spotted and Pied Flycatchers, frequently seen darting in and out of the open spaces. At night all changes and this area becomes the domain of Little, Tawny and Scops Owls, the latter instantly identifiable by the short musical whistle it emits from the gallery forest.

At the end of the itinerary you will reach the edge of an interesting lagoon with a number of viewing points along its banks. After having zigzagged along a boardwalk through dogwoods, ashes and willows, you come to the Palacio del Acebrón, where you should not miss the exhibition 'Man and Doñana'. Under the eaves of the building itself hang hundreds of House Martin nests and Barn and Red-rumped Swallows are also commonly seen here. The fields in front of the palace are good feeding places for Cirl Bunting, Meadow Pipit and Black and Common Redstarts, the latter frequently found here during migration periods. Don't miss out on the chance to climb up to the roof of the building for unbeatable views over the *cotos* (umbrella pine woods) and a chance to set up a telescope and watch for raptors in flight. At dusk during migration periods, European Nightjars sit motionless on the bare ground around the palace.

PRACTICAL GUIDE

Other access points: You can reach the starting point of the itinerary along the A-483 (Bollullos Par del Condado-Matalascañas) from Matalascañas and Mazagón. Coming from Matalascañas the left turn is dangerous and we advise you to continue on to El Rocío and turn around there.

Additional information: El Charco del Acebrón and its *algaidas* are part of the National Park Special Protection Area. The Palace has a permanent exhibition 'The Sound of Doñana' that describes the customs, traditions and ways of life of the inhabitants of Doñana, as well as an audiovisual display that can be seen in the palace's former chapel. Check the opening times before you visit: normally it is open from 09.00 to 19.00 in summer and 09.00 to 18.00 in winter

Transport: See the previous itinerary for details.

Water and toilets: There are public toilets and drinking water in the Palace, as well as drinks and snacks machines.

Wheelchair access: Most of the itinerary can be accessed by wheelchair, although there are some parts that are quite sandy. There is a lift in the Palace and access is via ramps.

Recommendation: Any time of year is good for this itinerary, even summer (but not at midday). This is an excellent route for wildlife photographers. We recommend you combine this route with itineraries 4, 'El Arroyo de la Rocina', and 6, 'The marshes of El Rocío'.

Itinerary nº 6

THE MARSHES OF EL ROCÍO

BASIC INFORMATION

Start: SEO/BirdLife Ornithological Centre (29S 723966 4112227)
End: Vera de Manecorro (29S 722669 4111861)
Distance: 2 km on foot
Map: SGE 11-42 (scale 1:50,000)
Municipalities: Almonte (Huelva)

One of the most beautiful wetlands in the National Park, the marshes at El Rocío are the natural gateway to the north-eastern part of the Guadalquivir marshes. This site is well known, above all because the A-483 road between Matalascañas and Mazagón runs along one edge of this sector of marshes and provides all who drive past with a view of the 'classic' Doñana.

The church of Blanca Paloma (the local name for the image of the virgin stored inside) is reflected in the waters of the marshes and two or three times a year hundreds of thousands of *rocieros* (religious and pagan 'pilgrims') converge on the village after trekking across Doñana from north to south or from east to west.

Anyone who has visited El Rocío in spring when it pulsates with life will be hard pushed to forget the sight at sunset of the marshes teeming with thousands of birds wheeling to and fro in the final golden rays of the evening sun.

DESCRIPTION

The marshes normally flood after the first autumn rains and continue under water until the beginning of summer; during July, August and the first part of September they are dry and apparently lifeless. The importance of El

The marshes at El Rocío at the end of summer © Jorge Garzón

The vera in the marshes   © Jorge Garzón

Rocío is due to the large quantity of birds that winter here and pass through on migration.

Start at the SEO/BirdLife hide: to the left, flanked by a line of eucalyptus, an extension of mud provides food for Ruff, Dunlin and even the occasional Spotted Redshank. Check out the edges of the mud for a possible surprise: one spring we had excellent views from this spot of a immaculate Long-billed Dowitcher.

Eastwards the edge of the marshes enclose an area known as La Boca del Lobo and you should scan this area and the far south-east of the salt-marshes with your telescope. The large cork oaks are favourite perching places for Griffon and – just occasionally – Egyptian Vultures. Easier to detect are the Red and, above all, Black Kites that also frequent the area. With luck, you may come across a Spanish Imperial Eagle in the eucalyptus.

With your binoculars check not only the nearby wild olives and eucalyptus for tits, warblers and, during migration times, both species of flycatchers, but also the vegetation near the hide for Cetti's Warbler and Bluethroat and the water's edge for the restless Meadow Pipits.

In front of you extends a large expanse of open water and this is a good place for ducks such as Eurasian Wigeon, Common Shelduck and Pintail, as well as freshwater waders such as Black-tailed Godwit, Avocet, Northern Lapwing and Black-winged Stilt.

A small islands protrudes from the water and here you should look among the Cattle Egrets and Black-headed Gulls for one of the Red-knobbed Coots that sometimes frequent the northern bank of the marsh. The nearby reed-bed is a good site for Moorhen, Common Coot and warblers.

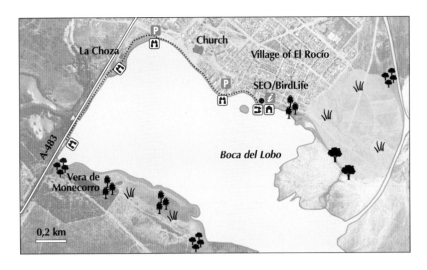

Leave this wonderful viewpoint and head west along the Paseo Marismeño, the promenade that runs along the northern edge of the marsh. The best time is early morning when the light, the cacophony of the birds and the lack of human noise reveals the most relaxed side of El Rocío; Greater Flamingo and Eurasian Spoonbill are common sights here.

Stop wherever you wish, although next to the esplanade outside the church is a good place as the wild olives here provide refuge for numerous warblers. Over the water, the rare White-winged Black Tern sometimes hawks alongside the much commoner Gull-billed and Whiskered Terns, while even in winter Barn Swallow and House Martins come here to feed.

Lesser Spotted / Spotted Eagle © José Antonio Sencianes

Greater Flamingos in flight   © Jesús Martín

Almost at the end of the promenade you will have good views over an especially bird-rich part of the marshes: the shallower waters here, exceptionally rich in invertebrates, attract waders, Common Teal, Garganey, Squacco Heron, Little Bittern and the occasional Kingfisher, the latter revealing its presence with its short sharp call as it flies swiftly across the *marisma* in front of you.

A little further on turn south, passing by a building decorated with an attractive mural of the marshes, and con-

PRACTICAL GUIDE

Other access points: You can reach the village of El Rocío by private vehicle or by public transport from Almonte, Matalascañas, Huelva and Seville.

Additional information: South from the Paseo Marismeño the marshes are within the National Park, the nearest information office being La Casa de la Rocina (see itinerary 4). At the end of the promenade you will find the SEO/BirdLife Ornithological Centre, although at the time of writing it is being rebuilt after a fire a few years ago. This centre is the best place for bird-related information, as well as for purchasing equipment, books and other material.

Water and toilets: Public toilets and water are available in the Ornithological Centre and nearby bars. There are also numerous restaurants and shops in the village.

Wheelchair access: Most of the itinerary can be followed in a wheelchair, although the sandy track towards the end may prove problematical. The SEO/BirdLife hide has an access ramp.

Recommendation: The worst time to visit El Rocío is midsummer (July and August), when the marshes are dry. Also avoid the mass pilgrimage of Romería del Rocío, when the noise and dirt in the village forces the bird to retreat to the other side of the marshes. Midday is poorest time of day for birds and overall the best time and place is probably afternoon from the Puente de la Canariega and/or the Ornithological Centre. We recommend that you combine this itinerary with itinerary 4, 'El Arroyo de la Rocina'.

tinue along a dirt track as far as a raised parking spot known as Mesón La Choza. Scanning the water's edge you should come across Northern Lapwing, Common, Green and Wood Sandpipers, White Wagtail and Greylag and the very occasional Bean Goose. Enjoy the show as the Common Buzzards circle overhead.

Continuing along the broad sandy track next to the National Park fence you will reach a stream, Arroyo de la Rocina, which you can ford easily (unless it is in spate). Under the bridge – Puente de la Canariega – over the road, it is quite common to come across Otter (*Lutra lutra*) spraint; Black Redstarts and Mistle Thrushes perch on the fence here when they come to drink. From here you should also take the opportunity to scan the trees along the water's edge for Lesser Spotted Eagle, a regular visitor in recent winters.

Itinerary nº 7

EL ARROYO DEL PARTIDO
(OR ARROYO DE LA PALMOSA)

BASIC INFORMATION
Start and End: Bridge on road to Villamanrique (29S 725800 4117502)
Distance: 4.6 km on foot
Map: SGE 11-41 (scale 1:50,000)
Municipalities: Almonte and Hinojos (Huelva)

The word 'torrent' (*torrente* in Spanish) originates from the Latin '*torrensentis*' and refers to fast-running water resulting from sudden heavy rain. In Spanish, the word '*rambla*', which comes from the Arab '*ramla*', means a temporary water course in an area of intermittent rainfall. In the case of El Arroyo del Partido, it is difficult to know whether we should call this water course a '*torrente*' or a '*rambla*'.

El Arroyo del Partido   © Jorge Garzón

Broad extensions of deforested land spread out on both sides of El Partido and abusive stock-rearing practices, aggravated by the torrential nature of rainfall in the area, mean that an enormous amount of sediment is washed into the marshes of El Rocío. Only in very few places do the remaining water courses retain any gallery woodland, although reeds and other types of aquatic vegetation are abundant in some places. The Plan Almonte-Marismas only worsened the situation by straightening the meanders of El Partido, thereby increasing the amount of erosion and quantity of sediment transported by the water course. However, it seems that one of the projects to be carried out as part of the Plan Doñana 2005 is the restoration of the original course of El Partido. Even today El Partido is one of the most bird-rich places in Doñana, although very few birdwatchers ever bother to walk the tracks that run alongside in search of interesting sightings.

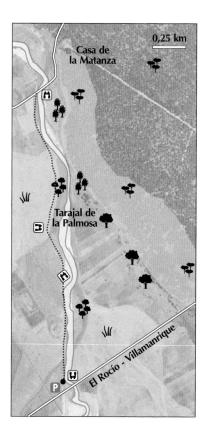

DESCRIPTION

Take the A-483 (Bollullos Par del Condado-Matalascañas) road to Aldea del Rocío and once there, continue on towards Almonte: after 1.5 km (just after the km 25 sign), turn right along a road signposted 'Villamanrique-Camino Agrícola'. This well-surfaced road passes between fields of strawberries and other fruit crops and takes you to a bridge over a tamarisk-bordered stream with parking places on either side of the road. From here, this delightful itinerary continues on foot and includes four stopping points.

The first observation point (**Stop A**) is from the road itself. In the early morning, there are many Cattle Egrets in the air over the surrounding fields preparing to head off to their feeding sites. Listen out too for the final calls of the Little Owl as it becomes lighter, while the trees and reeds of the stream are full of highly active finches (Goldfinch, Greenfinch and European Serin); Zitting Cisticola climb the highest reeds and Crested Larks run around in the sandy fields. Yellow Wagtails call as you begin your walk along the right-bank of the stream, heading north.

Follow the track along the top of the dyke for 600 m until you reach a point where you can walk down into the surrounding wheat fields. Listen out for the repetitive call of the many Corn Buntings. Just before here and near a house away to the left, look for a clearing in the vegetation (**Stop B**) and check the opposite bank for the holes

Pair of European Bee-eaters   © José Manuel Reyes

Calandra Lark   © Jesús Martín

dug by the European Bee-eaters that nest here. The shallow waters of the sandy river bed are ideal for waders and you might come across here Dunlin, Little Stint, Curlew Sandpiper, Ringed and Little Ringed Plovers, Redshank and Greenshank. This is probably the best place away from the marshes to see waders.

Continue and after a 1 km you enter an interesting area of fallow where birds such as Collared Pratincole and Woodchat Shrike come to hunt. Just a little further on after crossing a faint track that runs into the stream-bed, you reach **Stop C**, a patch of tamarisks known as El Tarajal de la Palmosa. The song of the Common Nightingale is easy to detect here, and the bird itself is often easy to see during migration periods. Look out too for Tree Pipit and Cirl and Corn Buntings; winter brings Grey Wagtail to the stream and the first warm days of spring reveals the sound of Red-necked Nightjars calling from the neighbouring fields.

On the other side of the stream you will notice that the forest is ever closer to the stream and after 1.7 km you will see a single dead eucalyptus tree with a White Stork's nest. Walking slowly and parallel to the stream on the top of the dyke, you get good views of the stream itself. In the surrounding fields, look and listen for Red-legged Partridge and Quail.

Just before reaching a bridge, a small chapel – Ermita de la Luz – becomes apparent on the other side of the stream. By day European Turtle Dove fly here, while by night this is a good place to wait for a Barn Owl to put in an appearance. **Stop D** is on the bridge (Puente de La Matanza): look along the course of the stream for Red-rumped Swallow, Marsh Harrier and Grey Heron. Gulls and Black-winged Stilts move around any patch of open water in the fields, Mallards fly overhead looking for resting sites and Night Herons emit their rough call at dusk as they prepare for a night's feeding.

Cross the bridge and return to your vehicle southwards along the opposite bank as untidy flocks of Tree Sparrows fly across the stream.

PRACTICAL GUIDE

Other access points: You can pick up the same access road in Villamanrique de la Condesa. You can reach Puente de La Matanza along the asphalted road that heads north-eastwards to 'Zona Recreativa del Arrayán' and Hinojos.

Additional information: Part of Arroyo del Partido lies within the National Park and is thus a protected area. One of the projects included in the Plan Doñana 2005 is to return the stream to its original course and to eliminate the dyke running along the left-bank. If this happens, return to your vehicle along the same bank. There are no information offices in the area.

Transport: An itinerary to be done purely on foot. No public transport.

Water and toilets: None.

Wheelchair access: Only the first 600 m of the itinerary can be followed in a wheelchair.

Recommendation: This itinerary is especially good first thing in the morning, when birds are moving between the stream and the surrounding fields. In summer, the stream is dry and fewer species will probably be on show. In migration periods, an early evening visit is recommendable, as many migrants roost along the stream's banks.

Itinerary nº 8

LA DEHESA DE PILAS AND EL CAÑO DEL GUADIAMAR

From Vado de Don Simón to La Compuerta del Caño

BASIC INFORMATION

Start: Vado de Don Simón (29S 748251 4118480)
End: Compuerta del Caño (29S 732435 4106780)
Distance: 30.2 km
Maps: SGE 11-41 and 11-42 (1:50,000)
Municipalities: Aznalcázar (Seville)

Although no part of the town of Pilas (Seville) actually lies within the National Park, it is still worth visiting Dehesa de Pilas, a magnificent site next to Finca de Banco that provides access to the northern part of the marshes and the pastures around Arroyo de la Cigüeña.

El Caño del Guadiamar – the remaining natural part of the river of the same name that was transformed into the canalised Entremuros river – is one of the most famous of all sites in Doñana and is a must for all visiting bird-watchers. This itinerary takes you to the best area for watching the Common Cranes and runs past the edge of the Hato Blanco rice-paddies. Unfortunately, your route also passes next an illegal dump for waste plastic that inexplicably has never been closed down.

DESCRIPTION

Begin the itinerary at El Vado de Don Simón, which you reach from Venta del Cruce and Dehesa de Abajo (Stop C of

Dehesa Boyal de Pilas   © Francisco Chiclana

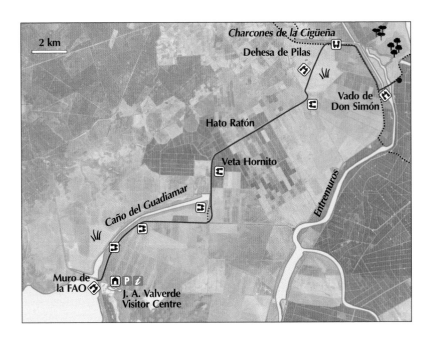

itinerary 14). Reset your kilometre counter to zero at the *vado* (ford or crossing point) that connects the two raised banks running alongside both banks of the Entemuros river. However, before driving up onto the far bank, cross the bridge over the river Guadiamar and stop (**Stop A**; end of itinerary 13). This is a good spot for Little Egret, Grey Heron and Eurasian Spoonbill, with the occasional African Spoonbill thrown in for good measure during migration periods. At dusk surprisingly large numbers of Night Heron appear in straggly groups from the tamarisks; Common Snipe are abundant in the surrounding fields.

The two raised banks limit the Entremuros river (literally, 'between walls'), which acted as a conduit for the disastrous spill of toxic waste that poured out from the mines at Aználcollar in 1998. Leave the *vado* and turn right, driving alongside the Guadiamar through dense vegetation home to Western Olivaceous Warbler and Red-rumped Swallow, the latter quite scarce in and around the marshes.

Continue along this paved road between fields and the river and after a left-hand bend you will reach another canalised tributary of the Guadiamar, El Arroyo de la Cigüeña. Soon, (km 4.5) you will come to **Stop B** overlooking an area of flooded pastures known as Charcones de la Cigüeña. As there is little space in which to pull over, you have to stop with care in an entrance on your left. These fields are frequented by rails such as Water Rail, wagtails and pipits (Meadow Pipit) and are also one of best sites in Doñana for Temminck's Stint, as well as waders such as Wood Sandpiper and Ruff.

Continue to the 5.6 km point, where you should turn left along a track that passes through a vast area of pasture dotted with the cattle from the nearby village of Aznalcázar. In rainy years small circular lagoons known as *derrameros* appear here. A kilometre further on (km 6.6), stop opposite a house

Whiskered Tern © José Manuel Reyes

– Dehesa Boyal de Pilas – and its large stand of eucalyptus (**Stop C**), home to one of the largest – and noisiest! – Spanish Sparrow colonies in Doñana. The sparrows bathe alongside Skylarks and Short-toed and Crested Larks in the dust of the track. Other birds to look out for here on the ground include the scarce Tawny Pipit and Little Bustard, the latter here in one of its last populations in the Doñana area. Much easier to spot are flocks of Pin-tailed Sandgrouse in the air, wintering Red Kites and both Hen and Montagu's Harriers. Large groups of European Bee-eaters congregate here before heading off to Africa, while on the ground unstinting groups of Spotless and Common Starlings and Magpies search for food.

Continuing along the same track, after 8.5 km you cross a small canal and then turn left. Just 500 m ahead, bear right after another bridge. Here (**Stop D**), the fields are ideal habitat for Calandra Lark and Corn Bunting, as well as for Common Buzzard, Black Stork (look along the canals) and sizeable groups of Common Crane.

After 12.2 km you reach Hato Ratón, a *hato* being the place where shepherds slept whilst away from home tending their flocks. The reedy canals on the left and right are of interest here. A little further on you reach the first of the rice-paddies and at a junction with a bridge on the right (19.5 km), you arrive at Veta Hornito and **Stop E**. Black-headed, Lesser Black-backed and other Gulls appear in the air, whilst the paddies here are frequented by Greylag Geese and the drainage ditches by Little Grebes; Ringed Plover and White Wagtails walk along the raised banks.

Pin-tailed Sandgrouse   © Jesús Martín

Cross the bridge and turn right to head for Caño del Guadiamar, being sure to check the electricity pylons here for the unmistakeable silhouette of the Short-toed Eagle.

Continue along this track as far as a pumping station, which marks the point at which the Caño de Guadiamar returns to its natural course (**Stop F**). This is an excellent site for Lesser Short-toed Larks, which are especially common in the *Salicornia* scrub or in the dust-baths on the track itself. When this area is flooded there is a constant transit back and forth of birds such Whiskered Tern, Red-crested Pochard and Northern Shoveler. In winter the vegetation holds Reed Bunting and the open water Little Gull, Black-necked Grebe and Red-knobbed Coot. Overhead, the graceful silhouette of the Great Egret is becoming increasingly common.

Return to the previous bridge (now on your left), cross another bridge over the canal and then turn right. Continue until at km 25.5 km you reach El Caño again. Here at **Stop G** you should search for Common Pochard, Purple Swamp-hen, Great Cormorant, Gadwall, Eurasian Wigeon, Great Crested Grebe and the occasional Ruddy Shelduck. This is one of Doñana's hotspots for rarities such as Pink-footed, White-fronted and Barnacle Geese; the much-observed group of White Pelicans that has haunted the area for a number of years often roosts here.

A couple of kilometres ahead you will come to a ruined pumping station (**Stop H**) and, in the shelter of the old building, this is a spectacular place to sit and wait for birds to turn up. You will not be disappointed by the coming and goings of the Glossy Ibis, Eurasian Wigeon, Common Teal, Pintail,

Great Egret in El Caño del Guadiamar   © Francisco Chiclana

White Stork and many other birds. This too is one of the most reliable sites for Marabou Stork, which has been seen perched on the electric pylons in the company of various herons. A little way ahead you reach El Muro de la FAO with the José Antonio Valverde Visitor Centre just to the left (see following itinerary). Turn right and in 200 m you reach the former sluices of the Caño del Guadiamar and at 30.2 km the itinerary ends. Return along the same route or follow Itinerary 9 backwards.

PRACTICAL GUIDE

Other access points: This itinerary can be reached from Villamanrique de la Condesa along the road indicated 'A Isla Mayor' from the roundabout at the entrance to the village. Along this road you reach the canalised section of Arroyo de la Cigüeña, which you should you cross on the ford and continue along the road to Los Charcones de la Cigüeña. Then turn right to pick up the access track to Dehesa de Pilas. From Aznalcázar this itinerary can be easily reached via Itinerary 13.

Additional information: Only the Caño del Guadiamar – the end of this itinerary coincides with its northern-most point – is within the National Park. The rest of the area is unprotected.

Transport: No public transport. The nearest bus-stop is Venta del Cruce. The track is in fairly good condition, although there are a fair number of bumps and in rainy years there can be a lot of mud.

Water and toilets: No water on route, although the José Antonio Valverde Visitor Centre 300 m from the end of the itinerary has a cafeteria and public toilets.

Wheelchair access: No real problems other than mud in wet periods of the year.

Recommendation: Any time is good apart from midday in the summer. The Caño dries up completely in summer and many of the birds mentioned are absent. Be sure to wear insect repellent at dusk in spring.

Itinerary nº 9

EL LUCIO DEL LOBO AND EL MURO DE LA FAO

From Los Madrigales
via El Lucio del Lobo
to La Cancela de la Escupidera

BASIC INFORMATION

Start: Los Madrigales pumping station (29S 748338 4115795)
End: Cancela de la Escupidera (29S 729854 4110357)
Distance: 27.3 km
Map: SGE 11-42 (scale 1:50,000)
Municipalities: Aznalcázar (Seville) and Hinojos (Huelva)

The Plan Almonte-Marismas disfigured the northern part of the Doñana marshes by diverting the natural flow of El Arroyo de la Cigüeña and the river Guadiamar into the Entremuros canal and El Brazo de la Torre. Furthermore, with the construction of the *muros* (dykes or embankments) much of the natural floodable marshes were left high and dry and then divided up into agricultural land (for example, estates such as Los Caracoles, Cerrado Garrido and Hato Blanco Nuevo). El Muro de la FAO split the Gallega marshland into two and water from El Arroyo de la Cañada Mayor was diverted into the interior of the National Park. However, the Doñana 2005 project aims to dismantle some of the embankments in this area and restore the natural flow of water so that the marshes – that at the moment only flood after rain – will at last regain their natural fluvial nature.

This is one of the most exceptional itineraries in the whole of Doñana and the number of birds and species of birds is at times overwhelming.

DESCRIPTION

The itinerary begins at Los Madrigales pumping station, which can be reached by crossing El Vado de los Vaqueros (Itinerary 14). Alternatively, the start-

José Antonio Valverde Visitor Centre   © Jorge Garzón

ing point can be reached from El Vado de Don Simón (end of Itinerary 13), by continuing along the road southwards on the right-hand embankment of Entremuros. Reset your kilometre counter to zero as the road becomes a track.

Birds appear almost immediately (**Stop A**). You are now next to the Corredor Verde del Guadiamar (Guadiamar Green Corridor) and this is a good spot for Gull-billed Tern, Common Coot, Squacco Heron and waders such as Wood Sandpiper and even Greater Yellowlegs, first recorded from the Doñana here.

Continue south-west along the top of the embankment on the right-bank of the Entremuros canal with the main wetland area to the left and cultivated fields (with Short-eared Owl) to the right. Keep an eye on the canal running parallel to Entremuros for Green and Common Sandpipers. After 5.4 km, you will reach La Bomba de la Sarteneja, a pumping station where you should make **Stop B**. Observe the birds that hunt for insects amongst the stones along the track: one of the commonest is the Short-toed Lark. In the estates of La Marijuela and La Sarteneja to your

right we have seen on occasions one of Doñana's rarest birds, the Long-legged Buzzard. Over the Entremuros river fly Black Terns and Sand Martin, while the open water is home to numerous species of ducks and even the odd Canada Goose. The vegetation along the canal is an excellent place to look for Great Bittern in winter.

Continue along the track, stopping where you see fit. For example, after 6.5 km at Cancela de la Curva there are excellent views over the whole of Entremuros and the birds that frequent the waterside. Soon you reach a large building, La Casa de Bombas, the main pumping station for the marshes, where there is an information panel next to the track (7.5 km, **Stop C**). Check the emergent vegetation for rails such as Purple Swamp-hen and passerines such as Reed Bunting, and keep an eye out overhead for Marsh and Hen Harriers, White Stork and Great Cormorant. Over the other side of Entremuros, the drier parts of the marshes are home to good numbers of Lesser Short-toed Lark and Linnet. The electricity pylons are ideal perching points for Peregrine Falcon, and the electric wires

The National Park from La Escupidera   © Jesús Martín

themselves fill up with Spotless Starlings at dusk.

At 11.6 km you reach a sign indicating 'Centro José Antonio Valverde, 10 km', where you should turn right and head off along El Muro de la FAO (which you follow to the end of the itinerary). Before the Doñana 2005 project removed the right-hand embankment of Entremuros and restored the estate of Los Caracoles, here you could continue alongside Entremuros as far as Lucios del Cangrejo. Nevertheless, you will look over Los Caracoles away to the south on the final part of this itinerary and Itinerary 16 will take you along the left-bank of Entremuros.

Continue along El Muro de la FAO, here separating the National Park (to the south) from the Natural Park (to the north), as far as a farm, Cortijo de Huerta Tejada. Stop here (**Stop D**) in this fascinating area: in winter a telescope will help you find cryptically coloured birds such as Merlin, Stone Curlew and Skylark on the ground,

while in the background you will hear the calls of the Common Cranes that feed here. The fences are frequented during migration periods by Common Redstart, Whinchat, Northern Wheatear and Tawny Pipit, and in winter Lanner Falcon is a possibility.

Huerta Tejeda is also home to one of a number of vulture feeding stations scattered throughout Andalusia that provide food for these carrion-eaters and any one of the three Andalusian vultures – Griffon, Black or Egyptian – may turn up here.

Continue along the *muro* and at 17.3 km, you will reach Casa del Lobo and opposite the *lucio* (shallow lagoon) of the same name. The marshes here are possibly the most species-rich point of the itinerary (**Stop E**). On the open water in and amongst the vegetation there are surprising numbers of duck (above all, Pintail and Northern Shoveler), not to mention groups of Common Coot, with the occasional Red-knobbed Coot, Whiskered and other terns,

Glossy Ibis © José Manuel Reyes

Group of Greylag Geese   © Jorge Garzón

Little and other gulls and the secretive Spotted Crake. To add to the picture, be alert for the groups of Greater Flamingo, Water Pipit and overflying flocks of Pin-tailed Sandgrouse.

You soon approach the José Antonio Valverde Visitor Centre (km 21.3), where you should park (**Stop F**). This centre is also known as Cerrado Garrido, given that this part of Doñana is called Los Garridos. From the viewing points inside, there are excellent views over the beds of reeds (*Phragmites australis*) and Great Fen-sedge (*Cladium mariscus*), frequented by both Little and Baillon's Crakes in migration periods. Purple Heron, Glossy Ibis and Little Bittern all breed here and are common around the edge of the lagoon. Beyond the first shallow *lucio*, extends El Lucio de las Gangas, frequented by Greater Flamingo and the rare Lesser Flamingo,

which we have observed here on more than one occasion. Cerrado Garrido is also home to one of Doñana's most sought after species, the Marbled Duck, which is commonly seen flying over the *lucio*.

After this relaxing stop, continue as far as a bridge (22.2 km), which is also the end of Itinerary 8. Keeping straight on you can cross El Caño del Guadiamar and look out over the vastness of the marshes of the National Park, extending from where you are as far as a group of typical huts (known as *chozas*) called Rosalimán over 1.5 km away. Along this section of the itinerary you will see again many of the birds you have already encountered, as well as huge flocks of Eurasian Wigeon (including the occasional American Wigeon) and in the vegetation of the drainage ditches, migrants such as Sedge Warbler and Bluethroat in winter.

In the rainy season the rest of the track runs through a boundless sea of habitat with in spring the flowers of pond water-crowfoot (*Ranunculus peltatus*) providing a beautiful carpet to the surface of the waters. The Hinojos marshes stretch away to the right, and this undisturbed area is frequented by the scarce Red-footed Falcon. This is also a typical place to come across Griffon and Egyptian Vultures, while year after year flocks of European Golden Plover and rather fewer Dotterel return here in winter. Stop anywhere along this stretch of *muro* (**Stop G**) to scan for perched or flying birds. Once past the *chozas* of Veta Perico (Chozas del Pastor), the broad Marisma de la Ma-

dre in the National Park comes into sight. Here, at Cerrobarba, winter-time birdwatching is like taking part in a great nature film, as thousands of geese provide an exceptional sound track to the end of a day's birdwatching. Amongst the thousands of Greylag Geese, this is the place to look for the rare Barnacle, Brent, White-fronted, Snow and Bar-headed Geese.

At the end of the itinerary you reach the gate into the National Park – Cancela de la Escupidera (27.3 km) – and have to turn around and retrace your steps, without forgetting to scan the nearby pinewoods for one of the Spanish Imperial Eagles that breed in this area.

PRACTICAL GUIDE

Other access points: Reach the Visitor Centre via Itinerary 8.

Additional information: This itinerary passes through protected areas, part of either the National or Natural Parks. All the tracks are public. The José Antonio Valverde Visitor Centre has an interesting exhibition entitled 'Los Caminos del Agua' ('The Waterways'), an audiovisual display that describes many aspects of the marshes and an information point and shop. Access beyond the Cancela de la Escupidera is forbidden without a permit from the National Park.

The name of the visitor centre is a homage to José Antonio Valverde, born in Valladolid in 1926, who died in Seville in 2003. He was one of the founding fathers of the Doñana National Park and a founder member of the Spanish Ornithological Society (today SEO/BirdLife). He and a number of other brave souls saved Doñana, one of the most valuable natural sites in the whole Palaearctic, from destruction. For those of us who had the pleasure to spend time with him in the field, it is a pleasure to be able to witness the fruits of his labours in the form of the endless landscapes full of birds that still exist in Doñana today.

Transport: No public transport to the beginning of the itinerary. The track is in fairly good condition, although there are a fair number of bumps and in rainy years there can be a fair amount of mud.

Water and toilets: Carry water, although the José Antonio Valverde Visitor Centre has toilets and a cafeteria.

Wheelchair access: The itinerary is well-suited for wheelchair users, although parts can be muddy. The visitor centre has been designed with wheelchair access in mind.

Recommendation: Any time is good apart from midday. The marshes may dry up completely in summer and many birds may be absent. Be sure to wear insect repellent at dusk in spring.

Itinerary nº 10

EL BRAZO DE LA TORRE
(NORTHERN SECTOR)

BASIC INFORMATION

Start: Compuerta de la Cañada de Rian-zuela (29S 750044 4120684)
End: Muro de los Pobres (29S 749357 4120254)
Distance: 4.3 km by vehicle and 0.8 km on foot
Maps: SGE 11-41 and 12-41 (1:50,000)
Municipalities: Puebla del Río (Seville)

El Brazo de la Torre is one of the former courses of the river Guadalquivir as it meandered through the flat coastal salt-marshes that were once subject to the fluctuations of the tides, weather and river levels. Work at La Corta de los Jerónimos in the 1970s and 1980s ended up by cutting this arm of the river off from the main course of the Guadalquivir. Today, it remains somewhat forgotten (even by birdwatchers), surrounded by rice-paddies, as it alternates between narrow channel, marshland and occasional extensions of aquatic vegetation and open water. The northern end of the Brazo has open water all year and is one of the main places of refuge for birds when the marshes are dry and the rice-paddies are not flooded.

This is a hidden corner of Doñana, full of birdlife waiting to be discovered. Even more remarkably it lies but a few metres from the most popular parts of Doñana and we hope that visitors will come here and help restore this magnificent site to its former splendours.

DESCRIPTION

Follow the instructions in Itinerary 14 'La Dehesa de Abajo and La Cañada de Rianzuela' to reach the beginning of this itinerary. Start at Stop B on Itinerary 14 and just 500 m further on reach the *compuerta* (sluice-gate) that controls the flow of water from La Cañada de Rianzuela. Opposite a dirt track heads into the rice-paddies: reset your kilometre counter to zero and head off along this track.

If you are here whilst the paddies are being ploughed, it will be easy to spot the differences between the Little Egrets

El Brazo de la Torre from El Muro de los Pobres   © Francisco Chiclana

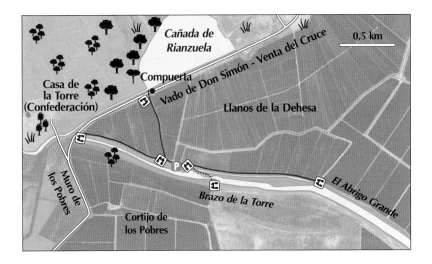

and Squacco Herons that flock to the area. The Jackdaws that roost in Dehesa de Abajo mill around in groups, Zitting Cisticolas buzz around in the air and Yellow Wagtails of all ages concentrate here in late summer before heading off to Africa. The Iberian subspecies *iberiae* rubs shoulders here with other subspecies of the Yellow Wagtail from elsewhere in Europe, while in winter White Wagtails with a few Pied Wagtails as a bonus take their place.

After 600 m you reach El Brazo de la Torre at a T-junction. If you turned right you would reach El Muro de los Pobres (the second half of this itinerary); for the time being, however, turn left and continue for 200 m more to **Stop A** next to a small hut containing a water pump. This is a good site for observing the flooded pastures and pools in the river bed that are frequented by waders such as Black-tailed Godwit, Spotted Redshank, Greenshank and Ruff that also feed in the nearby fields. The reeds hold Reed, Great Reed and Sedge Warblers (the latter on passage), while the first rays of the morning sun will reveal Penduline Tits and Reed Buntings. Collared Pratincoles

and Marsh Harriers fly low over the area and the presence of Barn Owls is revealed by their pellets, rounded balls full of small bones that these beautiful owls will on occasion leave on the top of the pumping hut.

Park here and look for a canal bordered on either side by tracks: take the narrower right-hand track alongside the flooded Brazo del Este with the canal to your left giving way to large expanses of vegetation. Keep your eyes wide open and pay attention to both sides of the track. You will almost certainly hear the harsh call of a Purple Heron just before it flies up out of the reeds and you may spot a Savi's Warbler halfway up a reed or bulrush stem. House and Sand Martins hunt overhead and numerous Moorhens will scamper away as they hear you approach.

After 400 m on foot you will reach a barrier that closes off the track (**Stop B**) at a place of exquisite beauty. On one side you will see large masses of reeds and a broad swathe of evergreen pastures and on the other El Brazo de la Torre, with its mass of islets dotted in and around the open water. Here the reed-beds are alive with large flocks of

Purple Heron   © José Manuel Reyes

Two Spanish Sparrows © Jesús Martín

Spanish Sparrow and two exotic species that have adapted perfectly to life in Doñana: the Black-rumped Waxbill, with its thin call, and the Yellow-crowned Bishop, resplendent in its black and yellow nuptial plumage at the end of summer. If you remain silent some of the shier birds will put in an appearance: Common Teal, Marbled Duck and Garganey, the latter during migration, and by dusk the Water Rails will be singing from the vegetation and the last Little Grebes will be making their final dives of the day.

Towards the east the flooded fields seem empty at first sight and it's not until you start to scan with your binoculars that you see that they are alive with waders and other migrant and/or wintering birds. Look out for Dunlin, Little and Temminck's Stints, abundant Meadow Pipits and at dusk the long shadows of the Lesser Black-backed Gulls that come here to roost.

Walk back to your vehicle and pick up the other track from the pumping station, passing between the central canal and the rice paddies, and head east along El Brazo. The rice-paddies that here separate you from La Cañada de Rianzuela extend across the plain known as Llanos de la Dehesa and are a good site in summer for Montagu's Harrier and in winter for groups of

PRACTICAL GUIDE

Additional information: The northern part of El Brazo de la Torre is unprotected and it is threatened by activities such as the illegal encroachment on the land, nitrification of the water table, the illegal cutting of the vegetation, to name but a few problems. Nearby is La Dehesa de Abajo (see Itinerary 14) and its visitor centre.

Transport: There is no public transport to the beginning of the itinerary and the nearest bus-stop is at Venta del Cruce. There are no problems involved with driving this itinerary, although it can get muddy and from the T-junction to the top of the embankment you may need a 4WD vehicle. The only nearby petrol station is in the village of Isla Mayor (CEPSA, open 07.00 to 23.00).

Water and toilets: No water on the route. Venta del Cruce is the nearest place with public toilets and drinking water. When the Dehesa de Abajo Visitor Centre opens (closed at the time of writing), public toilets will be available.

Wheelchair access: The only problem is the mud in wet periods.

Recommendation: In summer avoid midday. The birds present will depend on the cycle of the paddy-fields. Be sure to wear insect repellent at dusk in spring and summer.

Skylarks. At the 2.1 km point, you reach an obvious curve (**Stop C**) as the track bends to avoid a tributary canal flowing into El Brazo where you can turn your vehicle around. Find the highest point and admire El Brazo de la Torre in all but pristine condition, almost as it once was. This long lagoon – El Abrigo Grande – is a reminder of idyllic days long gone and has little to envy almost any other part of the National Park. At dusk groups of Glossy Ibis and Great Cormorants fly in to roost as Little Bitterns dart in and out of the reeds and wildfowl such as Greylag Geese, Gadwall and Mallard swim calmly across the open water. Few see them, but now and again an Egyptian Goose will put in an appearance, stimulating the eternal discussion regarding their origin.

Return from here on foot and then by vehicle to the T-junction from before (3.6 km). Continue straight on westwards for the final 1.1 km of El Brazo de la Torre: stop wherever and investigate silently any of the many flooded areas. At the end, stop and find a raised spot to get a full view of the whole splendour of El Brazo (**Stop D**). This is the end of the itinerary and one of the best places to view the waders that literally invade the rice-paddies after they have been ploughed. As well, the striking pinks of the Greater Flamingo and the blues of the Purple Swamp-hen mix in with the dozens of Little and Kentish Plovers and large flocks of Golden Plovers. With care and skill, check all the waders in search of one of the Doñana's most honourable of all visitors, the rare Pectoral Sandpiper.

And with the final rays of the setting sun printing an indelible picture on your minds, return to the road at La Compuerta de la Cañada de Rianzuela.

Itinerary nº 11

EL ARROYO DEL ALGARBE AND THE HINOJOS PINEWOODS

Old road from Hinojos to La Palma

BASIC INFORMATION

Start: Road from Hinojos to La Palma (29S 732700 4131452)
End: A-482, km 11.8 (29S 730614 4129391)
Distance: 22 km
Maps: SGE 11-40 and 11-41 (1:50,000)
Municipalities: Hinojos and Chucena (Huelva)

Despite never having been described before, this is undoubtedly one of the most interesting birdwatching itineraries in Doñana. It coincides in part with the old trail from Hinojos to La Palma del Condado and passes through a beautiful mosaic of traditional agricultural habitats. Of most interest perhaps are El Arroyo del Algarbe, a well-preserved stretch of fluvial woodland, the ecotones between El Arroyo and the umbrella pine woodlands that border the northern parts of the Doñana marshes, and Garruchena, a magnificent cork oak forest with majestic old trees. Other habitats include young holm oak woodland, pastures, vineyards and eucalyptus repopulations. This area is wonderful for observing passerines and raptors in spring, as well as for all kinds of birds during spring and autumn passage.

DESCRIPTION

This itinerary begins in the town of Hinojos: from the A-474 (Hinojos-Seville) coming from Aznalcázar and Pilas, turn off towards Hinojos and then

El Arroyo del Algarbe © Jorge Garzón

Rufous Bush Robin © Juan Luis Muñoz

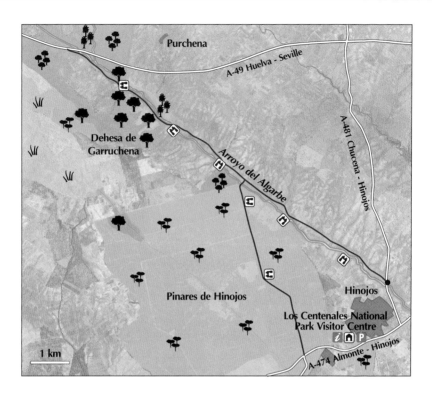

just before a petrol station, turn right to pick up the A-481 to Chucena (after having just passed under it). Head towards Chucena at a STOP sign and then, just after passing over a bridge over a stream, look on the left for the asphalted track that connects Hinojos and La Palma del Condado. Reset your kilometre counter to zero.

After a first kilometre of olive groves and cultivated fields, stop (**Stop A**) just where you see a stand of willows and a large poplar next to a stream on your left. Listen out for Little Owl in the nearby olive groves and watch for the movement of the Woodchat Shrikes, while Ravens and Common Buzzards fly off to the nearby pinewoods.

Gradually the landscape begins to change and the first groves of fig trees appear with the fluvial woodland in the background. This is an excellent spot during migration time and a good site

for seeing the exotic Common Waxbill. After 3 km, when the road approaches the stream again you will get views through to the pine woods. Here (**Stop B**), the fluvial woodland is home to Wren, Siskin, Penduline Tit and Common Nightingale, as well as Wood Pigeon, Eurasian Collared Dove, Song Thrush, Redwing, Azure-winged Magpie; at the appropriate time of year, Scops and Tawny Owls call from the woods.

Two kilometres further on near the farm of Cortijo La Albaraca the vineyards begin to become apparent. Look for a broad track (km 4.6) that heads left over the stream and into the pine forest: you will explore this area on the return journey. After a total of 5 km, you reach the third stop (**Stop C**), an open area with a number of new species for the itinerary: Hoopoe, Tree Sparrow, Quail, Rufous Bush Robin,

European Bee-eater, Woodchat Shrike and various species of swallow and martin. The nearby low hills are home to one of Doñana's most delightful raptors, the Black-shouldered Kite.

The road approaches the stream once again, passing between small fields and scattered buildings. At a bridge next to the first stand of eucalyptus (km 7.1) make another stop (**Stop D**). The vegetation changes from here on and the first large examples of cork oak appear. The ecotone here between the fluvial woodland, the eucalyptus stands and the fields is perfect habitat for birds such as Cirl Bunting, Common Chaffinch, Common Bullfinch, Melodious Warbler, Grey Wagtail and Red-necked Nightjar.

Heading away from the bridge, the surrounding landscape changes as you pass between a mature cork oak forest on your left and open fields and pastures, separated by brambly hedgerows full of small birds, to your right. This is a good place to get out of the car to walk and listen for a while for forest birds such as Green and Great Spotted Woodpeckers, Wryneck, Blackcap, Western Orphean Warbler and Blue and Crested Tits. Be especially alert for the calls of the locally scarce Rock Sparrow, Golden Oriole and some of the few Stock Doves that winter in the area.

A little further on, the road crosses the A-49 Seville-Huelva motorway and continues on to La Palma del Condado. Here you should turn around and head back to the track mentioned earlier on during the itinerary (km 4.6) that crosses El Arroyo del Algarbe and enters the Pinares de Hinojos pinewoods.

PRACTICAL GUIDE

Other access points: You can reach the start of this itinerary from the A-49 motorway exit to 'Chucena-Hinojos', which will take you to the beginning of the asphalted road near the bridge over El Arroyo del Algarbe at the start of the itinerary.

Additional information: This area is not protected and there is no public infrastructure except for the Los Centenales National Park Visitor Centre in the public park in the town of Hinojos.

Although this itinerary runs purely along two public rights of way (road from Hinojos to La Palma del Condado and track through Pinares de Hinojos), the surrounding estates are all private and permission must be granted before you take any other tracks.

Transport: There is public transport to Hinojos from Huelva, Seville and the nearby villages. The itinerary is feasible in a normal car, although after rain be careful crossing El Arroyo if the water level is above the bridge. In this case, return to Hinojos. There are two nearby petrol stations: 'Q8' in Hinojos (06.00 to 22.00) and 'Guadiamar' at km 22 o the A-474 between Aznalcázar and Pilas (06.30 to 23.00).

Water and toilets: Hinojos has all the services you should need; the water of Arroyo del Algarbe is not potable.

Wheelchair access: No problem for wheelchair users as the itinerary can be followed by vehicle. The short walks can also be followed by wheelchair users, although the sandy tracks in the pine forest are problematical.

Recommendation: the best time of day for following this itinerary is the morning when the light is most appropriate, although photographers may find the evening sun better. Binoculars are essential for identifying passerines.

Blue Tit   © Jorge Garzón

From here you have 5.2 km of track through the large pine forest to negotiate. After crossing the river (take care after heavy rain: if the water is flowing over the bridge, it is best not to try to cross) continue for 1.5 km through a young mixed forest of cork oaks and pines. Gradually the pines start to dominate and the undergrowth thins out and you end up in a pure pine plantation. The best tactic is to park and wander into the forest on any of the many paths, although the best area for birds is to the west of the track. Throughout this section you cannot fail to hear the calls of the Short-toed Treecreepers and Great Tits that are very common here. Eventually you reach the end of the track after a total of 22 kilometres at km point 11.8 on the A-482 (Hinojos-Almonte) road.

Itinerary nº 12

THE AZNALCÁZAR PINEWOODS
Montes de Propios and Dehesa de Tornero

BASIC INFORMATION

Start: Junction of Cordel de los Playeros and SE-667 (29S 745555 4129090)
End: Cattle trough at Cortijo de Quema (29S 742960 4126281)
Distance: 12.6 km by vehicle and 2.6 km on foot
Map: SGE 11-41 (scale 1:50,000)
Municipalities: Aznalcázar (Seville)

"... Forests of stone-pine extend unbroken league beyond league, hill and hollow glorious in deep-green foliage, while the forest-floor revels in wealth of aromatic shrubbery all lit up by chequered rays of dappled sunlight..."

This description by Buck and Chapman in their book 'Unexplored Spain', published in 1910, defines perfectly much of itinerary 12. The forests of the *montes propios* (publicly owned land) of Aznalcázar and La Puebla del Río are one of the most important wooded areas in the whole of Doñana and the over 12,000 ha of umbrella pine, wild olive and holm and cork oaks play host to, amongst other ornithological riches, one of Europe's greatest densities of Black Kite and Tawny Owl. This itinerary on foot and by vehicle takes your through these wonderful forests and their western edges overlooking the valley of the river Guadiamar.

DESCRIPTION

To start, head for the town of Aznalcázar (Seville province) on the A-474 (Hinojos-Seville) from Seville. Once at the roundabout on the outskirts of the town, take the SE-667 towards Isla Mayor. After 800 m pass by a sign to 'Las Minas Golf' and then after 2.6 km you reach the start of the itinerary at the junction with the 'Cordel de los Playeros' next to a half-hidden monument to the local forest wardens. Head *east* along the *cordel* (drover's road), resetting your kilometre counter to zero, taking care not to head *west* towards 'Corredor Verde del Guadiamar' and the AFREXPORT estate. There are no specific stopping points described in this itinerary as the best way to explore is to stop wherever you fancy.

You start off along a broad dirt track passing through a pine forest: note the first of many Azure-winged Magpies and chasing groups of Tree Sparrows in the foliage of the trees. After 600 m, the Cordel de los Playeros continues straight on and the track you should follow bears right. You are now in an area known as 'Los Aguazales' in reference to the three

The vast Aznalcázar pinewoods   © Jorge Garzón

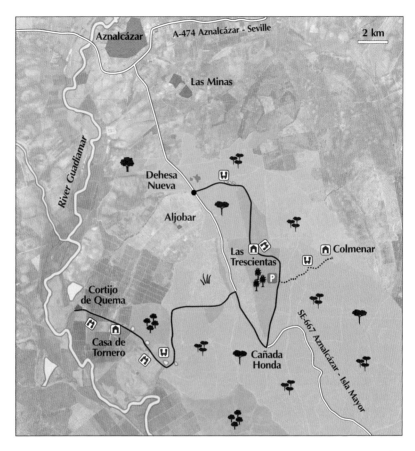

pools that form in autumn and winter on the left of the track. This small wetland is of exceptional importance for amphibians and many birds come here to drink. Look for Song Thrush in the pines or a Robin and Blackcap drinking at the water's edge as the echo of drumming woodpeckers reaches you on the wind. Soon the pines give way to eucalyptus (1.2 km) and the horizon opens up to provide views of the comings and goings of Wood Pigeons, Common Buzzards and migrating Short-toed Eagles. After 2.6 km you reach a ruined house – Casa de las Trescientas – equipped with a pond and a well that attract Blackbird, Common Chaffinch, Hoopoe, House Sparrow and, at nightfall, the ghost-like Barn Owl.

Anywhere around here is good for making a stop to wander and listen to the birdcalls emanating from the forest. We recommend you do so at km 3.8, just where a track heads off to the left and there is room to park. This track passes through one of the best preserved and least visited parts of the forest and takes you to Casa de Colmenar, another ruined house. In all, there and back, this diversion is 2.6 km and follows the track heading west slightly uphill.

Just 300 m after reaching the top of this small hill, you reach a point – easily recognisable by the small wild olive – where various tracks intersect. Follow the track that heads east with a large pine on the right and a small wild olive ahead. Walking in silence through the forest is best way of observing passerines such as Sardinian Warbler, thrushes and flycatchers; in the background European Turtle Dove and Southern Grey Shrike perform their characteristic songs. After 700 m along this track, another track heads off to the right and provides an open-

ing for scanning the sky for the here resident Booted Eagles and the Ravens that assiduously patrol this sector of the forest.

The rich Mediterranean vegetation here – myrtle, strawberry-tree, lentisc, *Daphne gnidium*, *Phillyrea*, lavenders – provide food and shelter for many wintering species of bird. After walk-

Tawny Owl   © José Manuel Reyes

Dehesa de Tornero, near El Corredor Verde   © Jorge Garzón

ing for 1.3 km you reach Casa de Colmenar with its three enormous red gum trees (*Eucalyptus camaldulensis*) and a large solitary holm oak opposite the house. At dawn or dusk this peaceful place is wonderful: Sparrowhawks call and owls and other crepuscular species appear from out of the depths of the forest. After exploring the area, return along the same track to your vehicle.

Continue along the main track until you reach a road – SE-667 (5.3 km) – at a place known as 'Cañada Honda'. Turn right towards Aznalcázar and for 1.5 km check the wayside vegetation

fortunately, part of this large area of scrub is being cleared to plant fruit trees, as you will see further on.

You enter the forest again and at 8.4 km, ignore the track off to the right that goes to 'Dehesa de Tornero', an ecologically rich and varied area that is incomprehensibly unprotected. From here on you will follow the western boundary of this estate and should look out, above all, for Spotless Starling, Corn Bunting, Woodlark, Green Woodpecker and Short-toed Tree-creeper, as well as Blue and Great Tits.

The pines gradually thin out in favour of the wild olives and you reach another junction where, just opposite a temporary lagoon, a less obvious track heads south-west into the woodland (take care to get the correct junction: the kilometre counter should read 9.7 km). Very quickly this track reaches the open spaces at edge of the valley of the river Guadiamar opposite a small stand of eucalyptus and on the Cordel de los Isleños drover's road (see map).

From here until the end of the itinerary you follow this drover's road north-west between the protected area of Corredor Verde del Guadiamar on your left and a mixed *dehesa* of holm and cork oaks on your right. Near here, to the right the first of three seasonal lagoons surrounded by ashes, willows and wild olives provides refuge for Golden Oriole, Melodious Warbler and the scarce Hawfinch. At 10.7 km you reach the second seasonal lagoon, where Long-eared Owls sit silently by day in the oaks in the company of groups of Crested Tits. This is also a good site to come to at nightfall to see the local Red-necked Nightjars and hear their curious repetitive song.

for Goldfinches and other finches feeding on the flowers in the verges. After 6.8 km, turn left along a track signposted 'La Tiesa' and notice the large area of scrub to the right. This is an excellent site for Spectacled and Subalpine Warblers, Northern Wheatear on passage and the scarce Thekla Lark. Un-

Black Kite   © Javier Milla

PRACTICAL GUIDE

Other access points: You can reach the beginning of the itinerary by leaving the A-49 motorway at the junction to 'Benacazón-Sanlúcar la Mayor'. Head through the town of Benacazón to reach Aznalcázar and the SE-667.

Additional information: The Montes de Propios de Aznalcázar and La Puebla del Río are not protected as such but have been proposed as part of the Doñana Site of Community Interest. These *montes* are commonly owned and are exploited regularly for their wood. The Corredor Verde del Guadiamar is a protected area and is part of the Andalusian network of protected spaces. There is a visitor centre in Aznalcázar (Buitrago) with a permanent exhibition.

Transport: No real difficulties. Aside from the main tracks, a permit from the respective administrative body is needed to drive the tracks in the area. There is regular bus to Aznalcázar from Huelva and Seville. The nearest petrol station is in Aznalcázar: 'Gasolina Guadiamar' at km 22 of the A-474 between the villages of Aznalcázar and Pilas (06.30 to 23.00). There is another petrol station in Pilas (Los Ventolines).

Water and toilets: None during the route and the last place to buy water and use the toilet is in the Aznalcázar camp-site at the entrance to the pine forests.

Wheelchair access: No problems other than mud in the rainy season. The track to Casa de Colmenar is firm and apt for wheelchair users.

Recommendation: Stop wherever you see fit and get out of your vehicle for short wanders. Binoculars are more useful in the pinewoods than a telescope. Botanically, this is also a very interesting route. The stretch of the track to Casa de Tornero and Cortijo de Quema can become impassable after heavy rain. In this case, return to the SE-667 and do not try and cross the stream next to the house.

A little further ahead (11.4 km) you reach the third lagoon opposite a gate in a fence and then soon you will see Casa de Tornero, surrounded by fruit trees, on your left. A few metres further on you drop down into a gully to ford a stream (take extra care after heavy rain when this ford can become totally impracticable) with the broad horizons of the Corredor Verde del Guadiamar stretching away to the left. Common Kestrels hover in the sky and in the morning Serins trill and the Quail call from the fields. Black Redstarts sit on the fence posts, while the power lines are frequent perches for migrating Tree Pipits.

Soon you reach Cortijo de Quema and its drinking trough at the junction of Cordel de los Isleños and Cordel de los Playeros (12.6 km): this is the end of this itinerary. Here, these two drover's roads merge and head off to cross the river Guadiamar at El Vado de Quema, a ford well-known to all those who participate in the annual pilgrimage to El Rocío.

Itinerary nº 13

EL CORREDOR VERDE DEL GUADIAMAR (NORTHERN SECTOR)

From La Dehesa Nueva to Vado de Don Simón

BASIC INFORMATION

Start: Junction of Cordel de los Playeros and the SE-667 road to Isla Mayor (29S 745514 4129111)
End: Vado de Don Simón (29S 748251 4118480)
Distance: 20.1 km
Map: SGE 11-41 (scale 1:50,000)
Municipalities: Aznalcázar (Seville)

One day back in 1998 a tragedy befell Doñana: the dam of a slurry pit at the mines near Aznalcázar burst and allowed vast amounts of toxic waste to flow into the valley of the river Guadiamar. The restoration of the parts of the valley affected and the areas bordering on the National Park have involved land expropriations and the

The 'savannah' at El Corredor in Matafuma   © Jorge Garzón

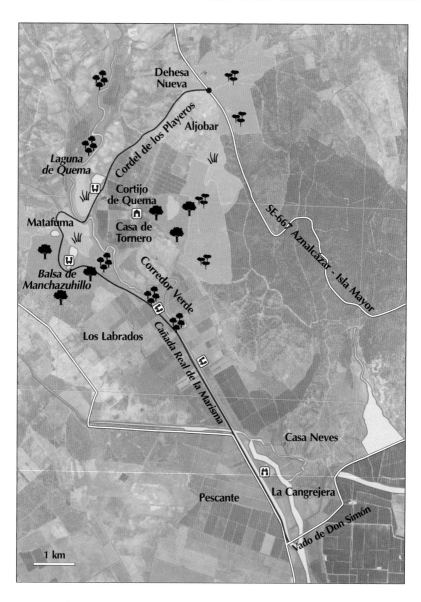

creation of a green corridor that today is ornithologically richer than before the disaster, when local landowners encroached knowingly and with impunity on the public lands of the valley.

This forward-thinking policy carried out by the Andalusian environmental department has not received support from local people, who, blind to the environmental riches they have on their doorsteps, continue complaining about the government's actions. Unfortunately, local inhabitants have yet to realise just how lucky they are to have such a wonderful site a mere stone's from their houses.

DESCRIPTION

El Corredor Verde del Guadiamar is the target of this itinerary, which starts from the same place as Itinerary 12. The first part follows a drover's road – El Cordel de los Playeros – eastwards from its junction with the SE-667 that is easily recognisable by two signs: 'Corredor Verde del Guadiamar, 5 km' and 'AFREXPORT'. Reset your kilometre counter to zero here.

To the sound of bird song you start by heading south-west between mixed woods, scrubland and fields of citrus fruits in the Hacienda Aljobar estate. Just after the start (notice the Dehesa Nueva watch tower and the mobile phone antenna) the broad track and the holm oaks along its edges are an unbeatable site for seeing thrushes, above all Redwing. After 2.4 km you come to La Atalaya, a good vantage point for birds of prey, and then begin to descend into the valley.

Drop down to the valley through peach and nectarine groves and at 3.5 km you will reach an irrigation reservoir – La Laguna de Quema and **Stop A**, next to the gate into the estate. This attractive reservoir holds good numbers of birds, including waders, ducks and other aquatic species. It is probably the best site in Doñana for Tufted Duck, which gather in this little-known spot in winter. Other denizens of this wetland include Gadwall, Mallard, Red-crested Pochard, Ringed Plover and Common Sandpiper.

Without leaving the track, head away from Cortijo de Quema and notice just a little way ahead a cattle trough, the end-point of Itinerary 12. You are now at the Corredor Verde: opposite there is a large ash with a White Stork's nest, now abandoned owing to human disturbance. Various species of raptor fly here by day: look out for Black Kite and Montagu's and Hen Harriers.

Southern Grey Shrike   © Mario Martín

Cattle Egret roost in Manchazuhillo   © Jorge Garzón

Just before reaching the bridge over the river Guadiamar you will see El Vado de Quema, a strategically important place on the pilgrimage to El Rocío as can be seen by the presence nearby of a shrine dedicated to the Virgin Mary protected by a vaulted roof and with a stool for worshippers. Stop on the bridge to listen out for Common Nightingales and Cetti's and abundant Western Olivaceous Warblers, while whole families of Red-rumped Swallows ply to and fro.

Continue onwards to pass over a cement ford and reach at 5.4 km the Cañada Real de la Marisma Gallega, another drover's road entering into the heart of Doñana. You are now in Matafuma, which, once a lagoon, is today repopulated with pines and small oaks and is a good site for Southern Grey Shrike.

Turn south along the *cañada* alongside the right-bank of El Corredor Verde. Just 900 m further on you come

to a seasonal lagoon that holds Grey Heron; the surrounding scrub is alive with Dartford and Willow Warblers and Chiffchaffs at certain times of year.

After 7.1 km you climb up to a low hill covered with large scattered cork oaks and reach Balsa de Manchazuhillo, a lagoon stretching away to the left of the *cañada*. This is **Stop B**, best at dawn or dusk.

This site has a certain magic to it, accentuated by the fantastic shapes of the dead cork oaks protruding from the waters of the lagoon that are used by numerous herons and Great Cormorants as a roosting site. Thousands of Cattle Egrets gather here in winter and at dusk the sound of so many birds can be heard for kilometres around. This too is a good site for Osprey, Common Coot, Common Snipe, Great Crested Grebe, Greenfinch and various species of sparrow and warbler in the surrounding trees and scrub. In January

Great Bittern   © José Manuel Reyes

2004 we recorded here for the first time ever in the Iberian Peninsula an Iberian Chiffchaff in winter. During passage periods the lagoon is lit up by the colours of hundreds of European Bee-eaters flying low across the water. Occasionally a Northern Goshawk will venture from the cover of the pines and provide you with a glimpse of one of our rarest forest raptors.

Just 600 m after the lagoon ignore the track off left that leads to Finca de Manchazuhillo and El Vado de Quema and continue south towards the flat expanses of the former marshland transformed into agricultural land and the broad valley of the river Guadiamar. On your left you will still have the fence to El Corredor Verde and from here on a clear winter's day it is possible to see all the way inland to the Sierra de Grazalema. Two of our pervad-

ing memories of this spot are seeing vultures from the breeding colonies in Cádiz province – 75 km away! – circling high, and one of the local Black-shouldered Kites hunting against a backdrop of the limestone mountain of Torreón de San Cristóbal.

The valley opens out towards the marshes with the agricultural plains of Los Labrados, where large groups of Skylarks gather in winter, to the west. El Corredor here is an interesting mix of pastures and fluvial woodland that offers exciting possibilities for birdwatchers. Aside from the continuous presence of large soaring birds, look out too for smaller species: during migration periods, interesting birds such as Roller and Dunnock stay awhile, while in winter Short-eared Owls and Peregrine Falcons hunt here. A little way ahead, the river has been canalised between lines of tamarisks and runs parallel to the drover's road. To the west on top of the low hills you will see the unmistakeable yellow-coloured Cortijo de Casa Neves; after 13.1 km you reach the bridge over the canalised Arroyo de la Cigüeña. In spring listen out here for the rough call of the Great Bittern calling to its well-hidden mate.

You reach here the road from Villamanrique and although this itinerary takes you straight on, if you turned right you would come to Los Charcones de la Cigüeña (see Itinerary 8) in just 400 m. Over the flood plain of the Guadiamar – known as La Cangrejera – and the rice-paddies of Pescante, Barn Swallows and Common and Pallid Swifts carve through the air, perhaps pursued by the dark outline of a Hobby. Stop awhile next to one of the tracks that enter the estates and look for one of our favourite birds, the Zitting Cisticola, whose characteristic call and hesitating flight will have accompanied you throughout the whole of this itinerary. In the tamarisks along El Corredor small heron roosts form that move from one site to another in different periods of the year.

After 16.2 km you reach the end of this itinerary at El Vado de Don Simón, another ford over the Guadiamar that connects to Cortijo de los Pobres. From here on, the canalised Guadiamar becomes known as 'Entremuros'.

PRACTICAL GUIDE

Other access points: From the town of La Puebla del Río you can reach the start of this itinerary along the SE-667 from Venta del Cruce towards Aznalcázar.

Additional information: El Corredor Verde is a protected area that forms part of the Andalusian network of protected spaces. There is a visitor centre in Aznalcázar (Buitrago) that was opened in 2006.

Transport: No major problems as this itinerary follows drover's roads and public tracks all the way. There are regular buses from Huelva and Seville to Aznalcázar. The nearest petrol station is in Aznalcázar: 'Gasolina Guadiamar' at km 22 of the A-474 between the villages of Aznalcázar and Pilas (06.30 to 23.00). There is another petrol station in La Puebla del Río.

Water and toilets: None during the route and the last place to buy water and use the toilet is in the Aznalcázar camp-site on the SE-667.

Wheelchair access: No problems other than mud in the rainy season. The whole route has good visibility for wheelchair users.

Recommendation: Any time of day (aside from midday) is worthwhile, as long as you take the position of the sun into account. Use your vehicle as a hide in open areas. A telescope and binoculars are necessary for what is one of the most species-rich of all areas of Doñana. After heavy rain fording Arroyo de la Cigüeña is potentially very dangerous.

It is also worth visiting El Parque de Buitrago, which can be reached from Aznalcázar along the A-474 to Pilas. After the bridge over the Guadiamar (2 km from the roundabout on the outskirts of the town), a sign on the right directs you to 'Jardín Botánico'. This public park is well cared for and was set up after the Aznalcázar disaster. Aside from many native plants, this is also a good spot to look for Siskin and Penduline Tit.

Itinerary nº 14

LA DEHESA DE ABAJO AND LA CAÑADA DE RIANZUELA

From Venta del Cruce to Vado de los Vaqueros

BASIC INFORMATION

Start: Venta del Cruce (29S 751348 4121348)
End: Vado de los Vaqueros (29S 749035 4115021)
Distance: 12 km by vehicle and 2 km on foot
Maps: SGE 11-41, 11-42 and 12-42 (scale 1:50,000)
Municipalities: Puebla del Río and Aznalcázar (Seville)

One of best-loved areas in the northern sector of Doñana is Dehesa de Abajo, a large estate well known to Spanish birdwatchers but not to visitors from further afar. The site possesses a magnificent wild olive wood, as well as important ecosystems such as areas of pure Mediterranean scrub, humid grazing and mature stands of pines. The site can also boast Cañada de Rianzuela, an area of exceptionally interesting pasture lying next to the pine woodland that floods every year from July to October, as well as the largest White Stork colony – almost 500 nests – anywhere in Europe built in trees. This spectacular area is easy to reach and the excellent wooden boardwalks make this site – close to other important sites – one of the most comfortable and rewarding places for birdwatching in Doñana.

DESCRIPTION

Begin the itinerary at Venta del Cruce, resetting your kilometre counter to zero as per usual. This *venta* (bar) is well known to birdwatchers and local farmers alike: at the roundabout pick up the SE-667 towards Aznalcázar along the northern side of the rice-paddies. Check out the nearby eucalyptus trees for colonies of Spanish Sparrows.

In 700 m you come to another roundabout: the SE-667 heads straight on through the pine forests to Aznal-

La Cañada de Rianzuela   © Jesús Martín

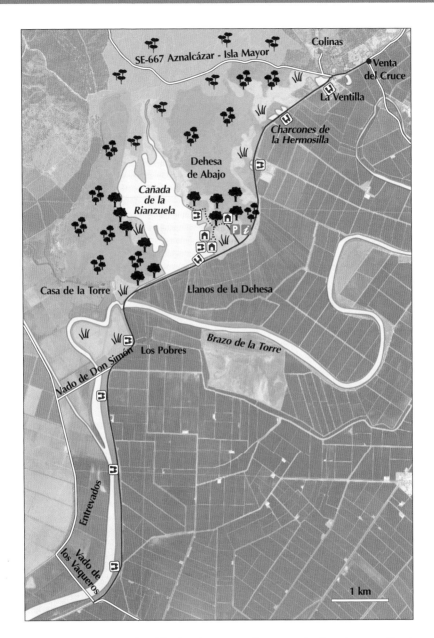

cázar, although you should take the left-hand road, the Carretera de la Confederación, that heads into the rice-paddies past a large agricultural warehouse.

Just 100 m further on you will see on your right a long fence of prickly pears that hides a small lagoon, La Ventilla, named after the travellers' hostal that once stood here. This lagoon, which sometimes dries up in summer, is home to breeding Little Ringed Plover; to the south-west of here extend the rice-paddies, which when being ploughed, attract hundreds of storks and herons.

Within 1.5 km the first of a large stand of tamarisks, home to many small birds during migration periods, begin to appear. Through their foliage you will see Los Charcones de La Hermosilla, a number of small freshwater gravel pits – now abandoned – that can produce interesting observations. A little further on, some of the gravel piles that are still standing are used by White Storks as support for their nests.

Next to the road and just before you reach some more pits, evidence this time of the mining that once took place here, you will see a number of small pools surrounded by tamarisks and willows that are home to Moorhen, Little Grebe and Night Heron, the latter using the tamarisks to roost.

The road approaches an earth bank just as the first wild olives appear: listen out here at dusk for the characteristic calls of the Little Owl. Now you are very near Dehesa de Abajo, and just as you reach the 4 km point of the route, you should turn right and head through the entrance arch to this visitor centre. Park and reset your kilometre counter to zero again (**Stop A**). Almost as soon as you start to follow the trail you will see on the other side of the open area that spreads out before you an enormous colony of White Storks, whose occupants mix with Black Kite, Booted Eagle and other birds in the air overhead.

Follow the wooden boardwalk to the right of a dirt track, looking out for Blackcaps and other warblers and Robins in the nearby scrub and wild olives. A little further on you have to cross an open area that is good for Great Spotted Cuckoo, Jackdaws and Song Thrush and Redwing in the winter. At the end of the boardwalk you reach a hide right opposite the stork colony: from here you can follow the dirt track towards a group of wild olives standing by the water's edge for excellent views of water birds and waders. Your telescope will reveal Red-knobbed Coot, Marbled Duck, Curlew Sandpiper, Little Stint, Ruff, Redshank and other waders, as well as Black and White-winged Black Terns cruising low over the water. Peregrine Falcons bide

White Storks and wild olive trees　　　　　© Jesús Martín

Red-knobbed Coot   © Jorge Garzón

their time, waiting patiently on a perch for the moment to pounce: when the falcon decides to strike, all hell breaks loose, as thousands of birds scatter in search of a safe haven.

Another boardwalk heads for two hides on the eastern bank of Cañada de Rianzuela. However, this is not the best place for water birds as the hides – facing the sun most of the day – were built in the worse possible place. Nevertheless, at the beginning of this boardwalk the views of the European Bee-eater colony in the sandy banks are unforgettable and birds will fly around you as you pass by. At dusk or on rainy days, hundreds of these beautiful birds congregate on the nearby electricity cables

and fill the air with their unmistakeable calls.

Return to your vehicle and leave the Dehesa de Abajo through the main entrance. However, just before leaving notice on your left one of the few monuments in Spain that have ever been raised in honour of an insect. The insect in question has been awarded the title of the "best defender of the marshes" and is none other than the *Anopheles* mosquito. It would perhaps be better to place this worthy monument right next to the visitor centre or next to the islet in the lagoon nearest to the road where it would be easier to see.

Once back on the road, turn right and in 1 km stop to view the *cañada* from the embankment (**Stop B**). In the foreground you will see a number of small islands where in 2005 a group of Gull-billed Terns bred and where a Mute Swan that somehow found its way here has taken up residence. Water birds abound to the left, where you should look for Greylag Geese, Northern Shoveler, Common Pochard, Garganey, Common Teal and Black-necked Grebe.

Continue along the road and after crossing the lagoon's sluices you reach an attractive extensively grazed wild olive *dehesa* (wood pasture). House and Tree Sparrows are abundant here, along with Common and Pallid Swifts. After 6.3 km, you reach El Brazo de la Torre (end of Itinerary 10) and just a little further on next to a curve in the road you will see a large fig-tree. Stop here next to the track that heads north to Casa de la Torre and Casa Neves (**Stop C**). Keep your eyes on the open plains of La Cangrejera to the west, part of El Corredor Verde del Guadiamar and home to Eurasian Spoonbill,

Black-shouldered Kite and Woodchat Shrikes, the latter often seen hunting lizards from a perch.

Soon the road will take you towards Vado de Don Simón (7.7 km); without crossing, continue along the dirt track (once the asphalt runs out) as far as Vado de los Vaqueros (km 12), the end of this itinerary. The area between the two *vados* (fords) is known locally as Entrevados and from this slightly raised point there are good views over the canalised river Guadiamar and the rice-paddies and fields of Isla Mayor, the name given to the area between the river Guadiamar and El Brazo de la Torre and also to the village that lies therein. This is a good site for wintering Marsh Sandpiper, Common Snipe and Little and Great Egrets, while the nearby rice-paddies produce interesting sightings of Black Stork in winter.

Retrace your steps, cross El Vado de los Vaqueros to Villamanrique or head in the opposite direction to Isla Mayor (see Itinerary 16).

PRACTICAL GUIDE

Additional information: La Dehesa de Abajo is protected as a 'Reserva Natural Concertada', that is, a site jointly protected by the Andalusian Department of the Environment, the Puebla del Río town council (the owner) and the local hunting society, who manage the site for wildfowl. There is an information centre, but it is closed at the time of writing.

Transport: This itinerary is easy to follow, although the track along Entrevados may be bumpy and muddy. The only nearby petrol station is in Isla Mayor: CEPSA (07.00 to 23.00). There is bus-stop at Venta del Cruce.

Water and toilets: There is no drinking water anywhere along the route and the last place for toilets or water is Venta del Cruce.

Wheelchair access: As most of this itinerary is by vehicle, there are no problems for wheelchair users. The tracks are firm and ideal for wheelchairs, although the boardwalk at Dehesa de Abajo is sometimes missing a board or two.

Recommendation: the best time of day is morning if you are looking west towards Entrevados. The afternoon is better for viewing the rice-paddies. The best idea is to use you vehicle as a hide; a telescope is a must for the large open areas.

Itinerary nº 15

CANTARITA AND EL BRAZO DE LA TORRE (SOUTHERN SECTOR)
Cantarita and Isla Mayor rice-paddies

BASIC INFORMATION

Start: Unión Arrocera S.C.A. (29S 751266 4112918)
End: Brazo de la Torre (29S 746410 4102048)
Distance: 15 km
Maps: SGE 12-42 and 11-42 (1:50,000)
Municipalities: Isla Mayor and Aznalcázar (Seville)

Aside from being the current name of the village once known as Villafranco del Guadalquivir, Isla Mayor is also the name given to the section of the marshes that extends between the main channel of the Guadalquivir and its secondary arm, El Brazo de la Torre, that lies to the west. Today the marshes have disappeared, the courses of the rivers have been transformed and, since the dark colours of the saltworts began to be replaced by the bright green of the rice plants, the wetland is now unrecognisable.

The beginning of the draining and transformation of the marshland began here in Isla Mayor, although curiously enough many of the ornithological riches of Doñana can be traced back to this very same moment in history. In 1974 a group of rice-farmers decided to supplement their incomes by releasing a number of American crayfish into the marshes, but little did they know that this foreign and extremely adaptable species would soon spread throughout the whole country and practically wipe out all of the Peninsula's native White-clawed Crayfish. Neither were they aware that this species would become the main source of food for numerous vertebrates, whose numbers have as a result partially recovered. The responsibility for

Brazo de la Torre at Cantarita   © Jorge Garzón

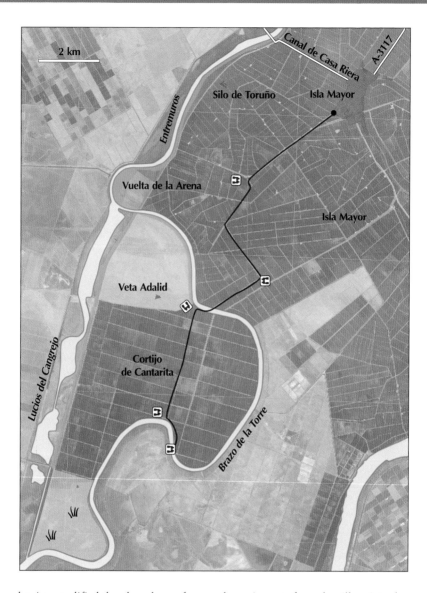

having modified the phenology of numerous species and helped their populations return to former levels thus lies with this exotic crustacean.

DESCRIPTION

Begin this itinerary in Isla Mayor, 13.5 km from the well-known Venta del Cruce (see Itinerary 16), where you should look for Carretera del Toruño (to the south of the main town centre),

the main route from the village into the vast surrounding area of rice-paddies. Once on Carretera del Toruño, turn right at the first roundabout and then at a crossroads turn left and follow a sign indicating 'Al Matochal'. Once on the road, the houses gradually fade out and warehouses and then silos take their place. Once at the installations of Unión Arrocera S.C.A., reset your kilometre counter and begin the itinerary.

The good dirt track heads straight into the rice-paddies and, despite the somewhat monotonous landscape, interesting birds appear straight away: Grey and Purple Herons, Little Egret, Lesser Black-backed and Black-headed Gulls, White Stork and Moorhen.

After 3.8 km at a canal next to a house, you should continue along the track next to a line of pylons that heads into the rice-paddies; Common Kestrels often hunt here.

After a while, the pylons cross over to the left of the track and, continuing alongside the pylons with Crested Larks, Meadow Pipits and terns flying across the track, head deeper into the rice-paddies. After crossing two canals, at 7.9 km reach a junction where to the right a track is signposted to 'Cantarita'. This is **Stop A**.

With judicious use of a telescope, you will have no problem finding all the birds that inhabit the rice-paddies here. Winter sees Common Crane, Glossy Ibis, Black Stork and Common and Jack Snipes; migration periods are good for Whinchat and, after the paddies are ploughed or have been harvested, look out for waders including Dunlin, Little Stint, Spotted Redshank and Greenshank. All year round, sandpipers and other waders and Common Stonechat feed in the area.

Continue along the track and pass through the San Ramón and Toruño de Juan paddy fields until you reach at 10.0 km El Brazo de la Torre, an arm of the Guadalquivir that today flows gently through these intensive agricultural lands. Next to El Brazo you reach **Stop B**.

Look for Purple Swamp-hen, although here this bird is rather shy because of disturbance from the rice farmers. Winter sees an abundance of Chiffchaff and, nearer ground level, Bluethroat. Reed, Great Reed and Savi's Warblers fill the reeds with song in spring, while Cetti's Warblers emit their explosive songs from a perch on any rush, reed or sedge.

Black Stork   © Jorge Garzón

Group of Gull-billed Terns   © José Antonio Sencianes

Just after crossing El Brazo de la Torre you enter into the rice-paddies of Cantarita in the municipality of Aznalcázar. Turn right at the first junction and then left almost immediately at the next to continue along the main track. This is a breeding area for Kentish Plover and on migration Little Ringed Plovers are common. Gull-billed Terns ply to and fro over your heads.

A couple of kilometres away to your right you will see the eucalyptus trees of Veta Adalid (see Itinerary 16). The rice-paddies to the west are frequented by the thousands of geese that flock to Doñana from October onwards: here, near the limits of the National Park, the geese use the paddies to feed and then take refuge from the hunters in the protected area. Along the track

you will pass Cortijo de Cantarita (12.8 km) surrounded by rice-paddies used by many thousands of wildfowl during the short days of autumn. Stop anywhere (**Stop C**) and try and identify all the different species of geese: the common Greylag Goose, the uncommon White-fronted Goose or the rare Barnacle and Canadian Geese. These rice-paddies are wont to turn up a surprise or two, perhaps a Ruddy Shelduck of uncertain origin or the smallest of all the geese that ever reach Doñana, the Lesser White-fronted Goose, a species that has been observed here on a couple of occasions. Look out too for Great and Cattle Egrets, magpies adapted to life in the rice-paddies and passerines such as House Sparrow and Common Starling.

Veta Adalid seen from the rice-paddies   © Francisco Chiclana

PRACTICAL GUIDE

Other access points: You can reach Venta del Cruce from Aznalcázar via the SE-667 to the town of Isla Mayor.

Additional information: the Cantarita rice-paddies are not protected since they are a working agricultural area. El Brazo de la Torre forms part of the Natural Park and the Andalusian network of protected spaces, although there is no infrastructure of any type.

Transport: There is a bus from Seville to Isla Mayor via Coria and Puebla del Río, with stops at Venta del Cruce and Isla Mayor. This itinerary is easy to follow, although the track is bumpy and muddy after rain. The only nearby petrol station is in Isla Mayor: CEPSA (open from 07.00 to 23.00).

Water and toilets: The last place for water is in Isla Mayor and the bars and restaurants in this town have the last toilets. There is no drinking water on the itinerary.

Wheelchair access: As most of this itinerary is by vehicle and the tracks are firm, this itinerary is ideal for wheelchair users.

Recommendation: The best time of day is morning if you are looking west towards Entrevados. The afternoon is better for viewing the rice-paddies and the section of El Brazo that lies to the east. A telescope is a must for the large open areas.

At 14.4 km you reach the well-vegetated Brazo de la Torre again. For a final stop look for somewhere along the meander where the vegetation allows you better views (**Stop D**; 15.0 km). Look across to the natural marshes that hold vast numbers of birds in winter. Here one winter's day we had the good fortune to come across a Sociable Plover mixed in with a flock of Northern Lapwings. Also a habitual sighting here is one of our favourite raptors, the Osprey, which uses the electric pylons as a perch for resting or for stripping fish. Lesser Short-toed Larks flit around the track and this is also one of the few places during migration periods that you might come cross an Aquatic Warbler.

The sight here on an autumn's evening of the unmistakeable silhouette of Eurasian Curlews and the wheeling flight of thousands of Black-tailed Godwits on post-breeding migration is unforgettable.

Itinerary nº 16

EL CORREDOR VERDE (SOUTHERN SECTOR). ENTREMUROS DEL GUADIAMAR
From La Venta del Cruce to Lucio del Cangrejo

BASIC INFORMATION

Start: Venta del Cruce (29S 751348 4121348)
End: National Park, Cancela de Matochar (29S 742326 4099999)
Distance: 35 km
Maps: SGE 12-42 and 11-42 (1:50,000)
Municipalities: Aznalcázar and Puebla del Río (Seville)

This itinerary passes through the southern sector of El Corredor Verde del Guadiamar and along the embankment that separates the area known locally as Entremuros from the rice-paddies of

The rice-paddies at Cerrao Chico. Stop A   © Jorge Garzón

The plains at Matochar © Jorge Garzón

Isla Mayor. This elevated track provides good views west over the canalised river Guadiamar and over the rice-paddies to the east.

This is one of the most recommendable areas for birdwatchers in Doñana since there is a good mixture of permanent water bodies and large reed-beds. It is also a good area for vagrants: two of Doñana's most recent rarities – Yellow-billed Stork and Western Reef Heron – were first seen here.

DESCRIPTION

Begin at the crossroads of Venta del Cruce, accessible from Seville through the towns of Coria and Puebla del Río. In the latter of these two towns, head towards Isla Mayor along the A-3114 and once at this well-known crossroads, reset your kilometre counter.

From Venta del Cruce, continue towards Isla Mayor along the A-3117 and into the first area of rice-paddies, flooded from the month of May onwards. In 600 m you will cross the canal from El Brazo de la Torre, where you should park and walk along the track alongside the canal (**Stop A**). Reed Buntings are abundant in the reeds here in winter, while the rice-paddies of Cerrao Chico are perfect feeding grounds for various species of heron, Black-winged Stilts, Yellow Wagtails and White Stork, the latter congregating here in good numbers on migration and in winter.

Return to the road and continue towards Isla Mayor, checking the rice-paddies as you go. There are few pull-offs; however, don't be tempted to stop in the road itself as local drivers are wont not to respect the speed-limit along this stretch of road. After a total of 5 km, the road bends sharp right at a bridge over an irrigation ditch. From here a long straight section of road leads between the paddies to the village of Alfonso XIII (9.4 km).

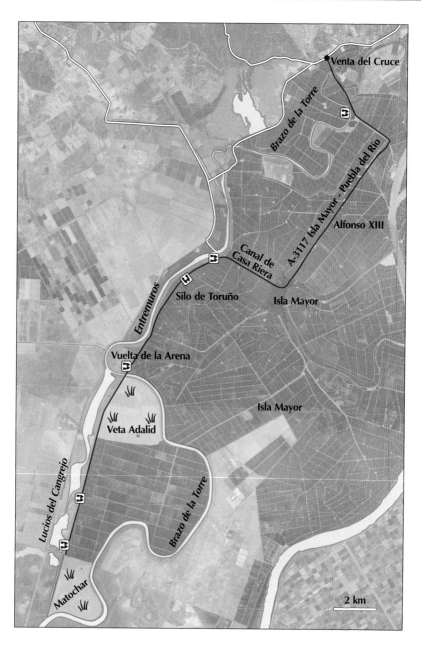

This village is surrounded by rice-paddies and has a small bar/restaurant on the road opposite the bus-stop. Where the village ends the rice-paddies begin again (**Stop B**): look here for a safe parking spot by turning left over the canal running parallel to the road. Pick up a quiet track heading south alongside the canal, where you will be able to stop your vehicle at will. The surrounding *tablas* and La Madre (the 'mother' canal that supplies the water to the paddies) are frequented by many birds and when semi-dry are especially good for various species of herons. In February 2002 we found a Western Reef Heron here, a species that is still occasionally seen in this area.

Return to the road across any of the bridges that cross La Madre and soon you will arrive at the town of Isla Mayor (13.5 km) opposite the CEPSA petrol station. Just 500 m further on you cross a small bridge and will see a number of palm trees in the town's main street. A little way ahead you cross a second canal and then immediately afterwards you should turn right as indicated to 'Vado de los Vaqueros, 4 km'. From here on the itinerary continues along a road run-ning parallel to a wide canal, Canal de Casa Riera.

A hundred years ago before the *muros* (embankments) were built and the virgin marshland was transformed into rice-paddies, the landscape here would have been very different. Nevertheless, despite the changes, this area is still a vitally important feeding zone for migrating and wintering birds. The Marisma de Isla Mayor is the name given to the area of rice-paddies between the river Guadalquivir and its tributary El Brazo de la Torre in which the village of Isla Mayor lies.

Ahead stretch yet more rice-paddies. At the end of the straight section of

Black-winged Stilt   © Jorge Garzón

Great Reed Warbler   © Diego López

road, bend left and then right to reach the eastern *muro* of the Corredor Verde del Guadiamar at El Vado de los Vaqueros (17.5 km when you reach the sign 'Doñana, Parque Natural'). The area of Entremuros lies ahead and from the track there are now excellent views over the wetlands of the National Park and the nearby rice-paddies (**Stop C**). Typical species of Doñana may appear anywhere here – from the rice-paddies to your left, the canal and its reeds or the open sheets of water. This a good place to watch out for Short-eared Owls at dusk hunting alongside the canal, or other species such as Marsh and Hen Harriers, Great Cormorant and duck. Passerines include Short-toed and Crested Larks, wagtails and Bluethroat, as well as many migrants. Other raptors here include Black Kite, Common and Lesser Kestrels, Common Buzzard and Osprey.

Continue sweeping leftwards southwest along the track on the left-bank of the canalised river. Stop wherever you see fit on the *muro*, keeping a very close watch on everything that flies in this area known for its ornithological surprises. After 19.8 km the track narrows somewhat (opposite the Toruño rice silo) and as you watch the Purple and Night Herons and Black-headed Gulls, you reach at 25.0 km El Brazo de la Torre (**Stop D**).

It is a good idea here to use your vehicle as a hide to avoid disturbing the birds. This site is a classic place for rails – Water Rail and Spotted Crake – and there are grandiose views east across the thick reed-beds, home to that tireless songster, the Great Reed Warbler, and the fence that separates the reeds from the grassy banks and pools of water; to the west gaze out across the broad meander of Vuelta de la Arena, one of the original meanders in El Brazo de la Torre. In the distance the Casa de Bombas (the tall pumping station correctly called 'Estación de Bombeo principal de la Marisma – Sector III') stands out and the area between this building and where you are now is known locally as 'Entremuros del Guadiamar', the canalised – that is, 'between walls' – river Guadiamar.

Once you start to leave El Brazo de la Torre behind, the rice-paddies stop and are replaced by pastures, scrub and a few cereal fields. The birds change too and here you should look for Lesser Short-toed Lark, Stone Curlew, Pintailed Sandgrouse and, in winter, Richard's Pipits. Collared Pratincoles feed here, above all at the end of summer when numerous different species of insects hatch.

After 28 km the rice-paddies reappear on your left and you will see in the distance Cortijo de Adalid (also known as Veta Adalid or Veta Alí), with its tall eucalyptus that is a good reference point in the flat Doñana marshland. A little further on your track looses it grey colour and narrows further; after rain it becomes clayey and may become impracticable.

At 31.3 km a small observation platform that once overlooked the former pools of Chozas de Cantarita appears (**Stop E**). This observation point gives good views over the nearby tamarisk trees, which hold numerous passerines during migration periods. From here you will also have views over part of the open water of El Lucio del Cangrejo Grande, where Kingfishers flash along the canals and Spotless Starlings busily fly to and fro. Just 300 m ahead, from the bridge over the canal entering El Lucio, it is easy to see Red-rumped Swallows and Sand Martins, as well as groups of Linnets, common in this delightful corner of the marshes and flying as always in small tight flocks.

Continuing south you reach the end of this itinerary at Cancela del Matochar, the gate into the National Park, after a total of 35 km (Stop F).

View the broad stretches of scrub of the Matochar inside of the National Park, where with luck you will spot a Short-toed or Spanish Imperial Eagle.

Retrace your tracks to Vado de los Vaqueros and then to Venta del Cruce via Isla Mayor. Another option is to cross Entremuros at the ford (*vado*) and link up with Itinerary 9.

PRACTICAL GUIDE

Other access points: You can reach Venta del Cruce from Aznalcázar via the SE-667 to the town of Isla Mayor.

Additional information: Entremuros del Guadiamar and Brazo de la Torre are protected areas, but have no hides or any other type of infrastructure for visitors. Fortunately, from the raised embankment there are excellent views of all the surrounding land.

Transport: There is a bus from Seville to Isla Mayor via Coria and Puebla del Río, with stops at Venta del Cruce and Isla Mayor. After rain, a 4WD vehicle is necessary for much of this itinerary. The only nearby petrol station is in Isla Mayor: CEPSA (open from 07.00 to 23.00).

Water and toilets: The last place for water is in Isla Mayor and the bars and restaurants in this town have the last toilets. On the itinerary there is no drinking water.

Wheelchair access: There are no problems for wheelchair users and all the tracks are firm.

Recommendation: the best time of day is morning if you are looking west towards the canalised river. The afternoon is better for viewing the rice-paddies. Use your vehicle as a hide: a telescope is a must for the large open areas.

Itinerary nº 17

LA CORTA
DE LOS OLIVILLOS
From the new course of the river Guadaira to Los Olivillos

BASIC INFORMATION

Start: Coria-Villamarta junction, between km points 9 and 10 on the SE-685 (29S 764964 4125931)
End: Stop A of the itinerary (29S 761868 4122885)
Distance: 16.5 km
Map: SGE 12-41 (scale 1:50,000)
Municipalities: Coria del Río and Puebla del Río (Seville)

There are still a few places in Doñana that, despite their ornithological riches, are relatively unknown and little explored. Once such place is the left-bank of the river Guadalquivir and La Corta de los Olivillos, an excellent place for herons lying at the confluence of the Guadalquivir and the canalised river Guadaira. La Corta ('the cut') was dug in 1971 to straighten out the Guadalquivir.

DESCRIPTION

Begin the itinerary at the Coria-Villamarta junction, which can be reached by leaving the main N-IV/A-4 road (Madrid-Cádiz) at exit 549 (P.I. Isla Mayor). Continue towards the industrial estate (on your right) and reach a roundabout where the dual-carriageway ends at Venta El Peregrino. Continue straight on along the SE-685 until between km points 9 and 10 you come to a junction: turn right and reset your kilometre counter.

At first the road passes through cotton and maize fields, good for migrant passerines such as Whinchat, Common Whitethroat and Common Redstart.

After 1 km you reach the new course of the river Guadaira at a bridge frequented by Black Redstarts in winter.

Ribera de la Corta   © Francisco Chiclana

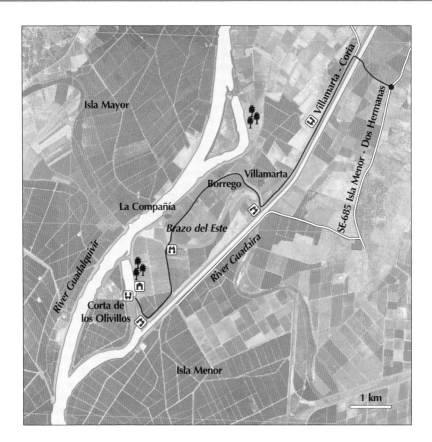

Although rather dirty, the river here plays home to a surprising number of birds, amongst them Moorhen, Common Coot and gulls.

After crossing the bridge turn left and continue along another road running next to the fields. Look out for the graceful flight of the Montagu's Harrier, Skylarks singing insistently, and Sand Martins flocking once the breeding season ends. The river Guadaira runs to your left, its course often followed by terns, Great Cormorants and other birds on the move.

After 5.5 km you reach a pronounced right-hand bend (**Stop A**) in the midst of tall eucalyptus trees, home to breeding House and Spanish Sparrows. During migration periods both Spotted and Pied Flycatchers turn up here and an evening chorus of Little Owls is guaranteed. The rice-paddies off to the right belong to the estate of Villamarta and are frequented by groups of adult and juvenile Grey Herons. A little further ahead, in the fields of the Borrego estate White and Yellow Wagtails mix with Meadow and Tree Pipits.

Continuing along the same track between eucalyptus you will treated to a revelation of colour during the breeding season for, aside from the Corn Buntings, Crested Larks, Tree Sparrows and chasing Little Ringed Plovers, the sandy banks alongside the track are home to dozens of pairs of European Bee-eater. After the breeding season has finished, spectacular numbers of these beautiful birds congregate along the

Fields next to Stop A   © Francisco Chiclana

power lines. As well, this is a good place to track down three of Doñana's more exotic species: Common and Black-rumped Waxbills and Red Avadavat. The river Guadalquivir is not far away beyond a line of eucalyptus to the right; from the sky comes the sound of groups of Collared Pratincoles.

At this point you enter El Cortijo de La Compañía (8.7 km) and 300 m on (9.0 km) you cross a small bridge over the tamarisk-flanked Brazo del Este, whose course here usually holds some water all year round. This tributary of the river Guadalquivir joins the main river a few hundred metres to the west and if you look upstream from the bridge you will see that this *brazo* (arm) has been blocked off by an embankment and has become in places a mere trickle. Stop by the bridge (**Stop B**) and look for Sedge, Western Olivaceous, Cetti's and Grasshopper Warblers (the latter quite shy) and Barn Swallow, all fairly common in this sector of transformed marsh. Eurasian Sparrowhawk hunt this area in winter, preying on the large groups of mixed sparrows that feed here.

After the bridge the tarmac runs out and rice-paddies and agricultural fields appear, home to Northern Lapwing,

Ringed and European Golden Plovers. Raptors are not scarce and include Merlin and Booted Eagle. After 10.3 km, you reach a small canal with a conspicuous group of eucalyptus where Kingfishers fish.

Soon you come back to the course of the Guadaira, where you should turn right. The masses of thistles on the roadside verges are favoured by many finches, of which the Goldfinch is the commonest. Out of curiosity, look at the banks of the Guadaira and note that, despite being almost 80 km from the sea, the river here is tidal. It also acts as a flyway for three species tern, Whiskered, Black and White-winged Black, the latter only seen occasionally during migration periods.

One kilometre further on (11.3 km), the track turns right, climbs a short ramp and reaches the top of an embankment, the northern *muro* of La Corta de Los Olivillos. These *muros* and the tracks that run along then were created when the virgin marshes were transformed into rice-paddies. Stop here (**Stop C**) and enjoy the view: below an island covered in reeds harbours a spectacular heronry that owes it size to its position at the confluence of the Guadalquivir and Guadaira rivers.

Squacco Heron © José Manuel Reyes

Collared Pratincole   © Jorge Garzón

Squacco and Night Herons and Cattle and Little Egrets come and go and there is always the chance of seeing the rare Western Reef Heron that visits this corner of Doñana on occasions. Water Rail are also fairly easily seen and heard and the extravagant Sacred Ibis, of unknown origin, may also turn up in one of the groups of Glossy Ibis that frequent the area. Keen photographers

PRACTICAL GUIDE

Other access points: You can reach the bridge over the river Guadaira and the road parallel to the river from Coria del Río: cross the Guadalquivir on the *barcaza* (small car and passenger ferry that starts operating at 06.00), and once across continue a further 5 km to the bridge at the starting point of the itinerary.

Additional information: inexplicably La Corta de los Olivillos is unprotected and is subject to disturbance, above all from local rice farmers. There a small semi-ruined hide under the eucalyptus trees next to the lagoon that can be reached along the path next to the gate at Stop D.

Transport: There is no public transport to the start of this itinerary. After rain a 4WD vehicle is recommended from Stop B onwards. The nearest petrol station is in Coria del Río, although you do have to cross the river on the *barcaza* to get there.

Water and toilets: The last toilets and water are at Venta El Peregrino. There is no water along the itinerary and you should not drink water from the drainage channels, however clean it looks (the chemical pesticides and fertilisers used here have no colour).

Wheelchair access: No real problems other than after rain. There is no wheelchair access to the hide.

Recommendation: Although good all day, we especially recommend the morning to visit this sites, above all from the gate at Stop D. The afternoon light can be spectacular, but also makes viewing the heronry on the island difficult as you are looking straight into the setting sun. Telescopes and binoculars are essential.

should wait until sunset for the rosy dusk light to illuminate the heronry and the Marsh Harriers that come here to roost.

At 11.8 km, just 500 further on, stop next to a metal gate (**Stop D**) at the side of a long line of eucalyptus trees that runs alongside a large sheet of water. This is the old course of the river and is a good site for water birds. Walk along its banks under the clouds of House Martins that come here to feed, looking out for diving ducks such as Red-crested Pochard, Common Pochard, Tufted Ducks and even Greater Scaup, dabbling ducks such as Gadwall, Pintail, Mallard, Northern Shoveler and Eurasian Wigeon and Great Crested and Black-necked Grebes. Osprey and Peregrine perch in the eucalyptus trees and this is one of the few accessible places in the marshes in autumn and winter where you can see the singular White-headed Duck or maybe even a Ruddy Shelduck.

Return to your vehicle and retrace your steps, although once back at Stop C you can continue all the way back alongside the river Guadaira to end this circuit at Stop A (16.5 km).

Itinerary nº 18

EL BRAZO DEL ESTE I
*From La Cascajera
to El Caño de la Vera*

BASIC INFORMATION
Start: Coria-Villamarta junction, between km points 9 and 10 on the SE-685 (29S 764964 4125931)
End: Caño de la Vera (30S 233724 4119157)
Distance: 15.3 km
Map: SGE 12-41 (scale 1:50,000)
Municipalities: Coria del Río, Dos Hermanas and Puebla del Río (Seville)

Over the last 300 years numerous meanders of the impressive river Guadalquivir have been eliminated – although none since the mid-twentieth century – to improve navigation upstream to Seville: the 127 km that once separated Seville from the sea by river have been reduced today to just 77 km. The 'new' cuts at La Isleta and Fernandina have left the river much straighter and sluice-gates now control the waters of the river. El Brazo del Este is one of the former tributaries of the

Brazo del Este. El Conde Chico © Francisco Chiclana

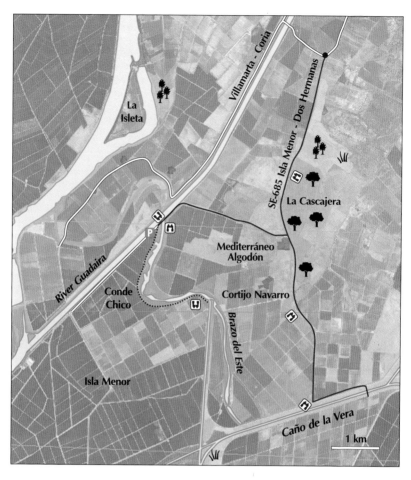

Guadalquivir and this too has been canalised and is no longer tidal. Furthermore, it is now cut off by an embankment of the Guadalquivir and its water levels thus depend on rainfall and run-off from the surrounding rice-paddies. However, large areas of open water form here thanks to the clayey alluvial soil and there are thick belts of natural vegetation (reeds, bulrushes, sedge, etc.) and vast extensions of paddy-fields; this is thus one of the most species-rich areas of Doñana.

DESCRIPTION

Begin the itinerary at the Coria-Villamarta junction, which can be reached by leaving the main N-IV/A-4 road (Madrid-Cádiz) at exit 549 (P.I. Isla Mayor). Continue towards the industrial estate (on your right) and reach a roundabout where the dual-carriageway ends at Venta El Peregrino. Continue straight on along the SE-685 until between km points 9 and 10 you come to a junction. This is the same point as the beginning of Itinerary 17: reset the kilometre counter and head south, straight on along the SE-685.

Soon you pass through the first fields – cotton and other crops – that harbour an abundance of wagtails and pipits and other passerines. The electric posts on the left are a favourite perching

Group of White Storks in winter   © Jorge Garzón

place for Booted Eagles, one of the commonest raptors in this part of Doñana. Two kilometres further on the road passes through a stand of eucalyptus that mark the entrance to the wild olive woodland of the La Cascajera estate that lies to your left. A kilometre further on, make your first stop (**Stop A**) next to the gate into the estate. Stands of wild olives of such proportions are not common in Doñana and their verdant crowns provide shelter for a wide range of small birds – Sardinian, Subalpine and Garden Warblers, thrushes such as Robin and Blackbird and various finches including Greenfinch and Serin. Other birds that you should come across easily here include Hoopoe, Green Woodpecker, Golden Oriole, Woodlark, Great Tit and, at dusk, Red-necked Nightjar; during migration periods this is perhaps the best site in Doñana for one of the country's most beautiful birds, the Roller.

As night begins to fall it's worth waiting here for the unmistakeable sound of the Eagle Owl, the largest owl in the Peninsula. Winter brings Black Storks to the area, and you should search the agricultural areas off to the west for one of these graceful birds feeding in and amongst the groups of White Storks.

At 3.9 km you reach a cotton warehouse called 'Mediterráneo Algodón': remember this spot as it is where you return to at the end of this itinerary. Bend right and continue along the asphalted road as the woodland thins out into pastures dotted with just the odd wild olive tree here and there, excellent perching posts for many Woodchat Shrikes at the end of summer. At 6.3 km you reach the course of the river Guadaira just after passing a line of eucalyptus trees.

Look ahead and in 400 m you will see the course of El Brazo del Este on the left, its natural connection to the river truncated by the *muro* that provides the base for the track you are on. On the far side of El Brazo on its western bank, the track begins that you will walk for the next part of this itinerary. Park (**Stop B**; 7.0 km) and observe this

Greenshank   © Mario Martín

interesting wetland. The call of the Penduline Tit will be apparent and in the pools of El Brazo you should look out for Greenshank, Common Snipe, Greater Flamingo and the scarce Marbled Duck and Temminck's Stint.

Begin to walk along the bank along a track known as Conde Chico, flanked to the right by the rice-paddies of Isla Menor that extend between the Guadalquivir and El Brazo del Este. On the two kilometres of this path a multitude of birds will reveal themselves: especially common is the Purple Swamphen, while Pallid and Alpine Swifts fly overhead at great height. There are no particular places to stop as you will come across almost anywhere species such as White Wagtail, Bluethroat, Common Stonechat, Savi's Warbler, Little Bittern, Squacco Heron and Eurasian and even African Spoonbills, the latter a rare species that turns up here now and again.

When you reach the end of the track (easily recognisable by the drainage ditch that crosses El Brazo here), return to your vehicle and drive back to the crossroads next to the cotton warehouse (10.1 km). Turn right towards 'Poblado Adriano' with the warehouse on your right.

The track heads south with wild olive woodland on your left and then fields and fallow on your right a little way ahead. After passing a stand of eucalyptus, next to some raised water conduits you should hear both Red-legged Partridge and Quail. Continuing to head south, this track will take you to the northern *muro* (a raised embankment that can be driven along) of El Caño de la Vera (**Stop C**; 13.8 km).

From here look over the saltworts and glasswarts that cover the course of this *caño*, where the scarce Pin-tailed Sandgrouse and other interesting species such as Collared Pratincole, Short-toed Lark, Spanish Sparrow and Northern and Black-eared Wheatears can be found. Barn and Short-eared Owls frequent this site and the abun-

Purple Swamp-hen   © Mario Martín

PRACTICAL GUIDE

Other access points: You can reach the junction of the Coria-Villamarta road from Coria by crossing the Guadalquivir on the *barcaza* (small car and passenger ferry that starts operating at 06.00) . Once across you have to continue a further 5 km to the junction with the SE-685.

Additional information: Despite being a protected area, this site has no infrastructure for birdwatchers. The extensive network of *muros* (raised platforms that act as tracks) make getting around easy and are ideal places birdwatching. The official name of this site is Paraje Natural Brazo del Este and is part of the Andalusian network of protected spaces. It has also been recently declared a RAMSAR site.

Transport: In winter take care after rain, although the tracks are generally in good condition. There are petrol stations open 24 hours a day in the nearby towns. There is no public transport.

Water and toilets: Water can be bought in Venta El Peregrino, where there are also toilets.

Wheelchair access: There are no complications for wheelchair users since all the stops are in areas with broad, well-made tracks. Mud in the wet season may, however, be somewhat of a problem.

Recommendation: There are excellent observations to be made here all year round. Telescopes are very useful. Take care not to get lost in the rather confusing network of tracks.

Other places of interest: La Laguna de la Mejorada (known locally as Laguna de Diego Puertas) is an old gravel pit lying next to the Canal del Bajo Guadalquivir on the outskirts of the town of Los Palacios y Villafranca. This is a highly recommendable site as it is an ideal place for seeing two interesting species, Rufous Bush Robin and Western Olivaceous Warbler. In winter, the vegetation around the lagoon holds one of the biggest heron roosts in the whole of Spain.

dance of Yellow Wagtails provide an opportunity to compare some of this species' different races during migration periods.

After this stop, continue left along the *muro* with El Caño de la Vera to your right. Stop whenever you see something of interest: migration periods after rain are the best, when pools of water form in El Caño and Common Redshank and Wood and Green Sandpipers, the latter commoner in the smaller secondary *caños*, come to feed.

Within just over a kilometre, follow a track off to the right that descends and crosses the Caño before climbing up its southern *muro* (15.3 km; **Stop D**).

Common Sandpipers are easy to see here, while Ringed Plovers patrol the banks of El Caño. In winter Calandra Larks appear here, along with various species of gulls – above all the Lesser Black-backed Gull – who come to feed on the American Crayfish.

This itinerary ends here: if you continue along the southern wall of El Caño you will reach the town of Los Palacios y Villafranca.

EL BRAZO DEL ESTE II
*From Chapatales
to the Isla Menor rice-paddies
and El Reboso*

BASIC INFORMATION

Start: Junction in the road from Los Palacios to Pinzón (29S 732700 4131452)
End: El Reboso rice silos (30S 238623 4116708)
Distance: 16 km
Map: SGE 12-42 (scale 1:50,000)
Municipalities: Los Palacios y Villafranca, Puebla del Río and Utrera (Seville)

This itinerary is a continuation of the previous itinerary (Itinerary 18 'El Brazo del Este I') and concentrates on the south-western sector of El Brazo del Este.

DESCRIPTION

To reach the start of this itinerary take the main N-IV Madrid-Cádiz road towards Cádiz and when on the Los Palacios y Villafranca bypass, look for an

Brazo del Este. La Margazuela   © Francisco Chiclana

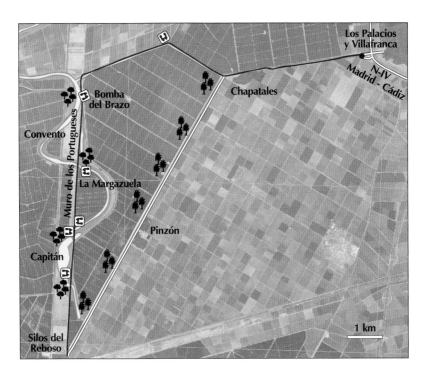

exit (km 568.8) indicated 'Los Palacios, Chapatales y Pinzón'. Turn off and almost immediately you will reach a junction with a STOP sign next to a warehouse: turn left along the road to Pinzón and Chapatales and reset you kilometre counter to zero.

After 1.5 km you will pass by the village of Chapatales on your left and just afterwards turn right on a dirt track that crosses a small bridge over a canal. An obvious line of eucalyptus trees make the junction very visible. You begin to pass through the typical rice-paddies of Doñana, created out of the transformation of the marshes and populated by herons and *gallos azules* (literally, 'blue hens'), the local name for the Purple Swamp-hen.

The first stop is at km 5.5 (**Stop A**) in an area of rice-paddies that, when freshly harvested and ploughed at the end of summer, attract numerous gulls, including Lesser Black-backed and Black-headed, as well as Black Stork in winter (also known locally as the *dama negra*, the 'black lady'!).

Immediately after crossing over a canal, turn left on a dirt track. After 3 km (8.8 km in total) you will come to a broader track flank by a line of electricity posts. Follow for just 50 m and you will come to a large pumping station – La Bomba del Brazo (**Stop B**). On winter afternoons it is worth checking the posts to the right for perched Peregrine Falcons. This is also a great place for seeing Great Spotted Cuckoo during migration and for wildfowl such as Common Teal and Garganey. Along the banks of the rice-paddies look out for passage waders such as Ruff, Wood Sandpiper, Dunlin and Little Stint, while the stands of tamarisks harbour variable numbers of Cattle and Little Egrets and Night Heron. Squacco Herons often roost here by day and Great Egrets wander around next to groups of Common and Spotless Starlings; half of Doñana's records of Rose-coloured Starling are from here.

Once over the canal, continue along a wide dirt track with El Brazo del Este to the right. This raised track, known as El Muro de los Portugueses and built as part of the project to transform the virgin marshes into rice-paddies, is frequented by farm vehicles and heads due south cutting off the meanders of the former course of El Brazo del Este. After 10.7 km the rice-paddies disappear and the typical vegetation of the Doñana wetlands reappears. This spot is known as La Margazuela after a nearby farm and at an intersection of the embankment and the Brazo you should make **Stop C.**

This is an exceptional birdwatching spot due to the mosaic of open water and patches of reeds, bulrushes and rushes that constitute the dominant vegetation here. Eurasian Spoonbill, Little Bittern, Black, Whiskered and Gull-billed Terns, Purple Swamp-hen and Reed and Great Reed Warblers are some of the species you should find here, as well as the delicate Little Tern, an occasional breeder in this sector of Doñana. At the end of summer, the exotic Yellow-crowned Bishop shows

Rice plants   © Francisco Chiclana

Savi's Warbler © Jesús Martín

off its fine black and yellow breeding plumage from a reedy stem. Dusk is a good time for spotting the shy Spotted Crake amongst the vegetation and if water levels are not too high there will be plenty of waders including Temminck's Stints feeding here.

Continuing south you come to an area of virgin marshland frequented by Stone Curlew and Short-toed Lark, as

Marbled Duck © Jesús Martín

well as by groups of Spanish Sparrow, Corn Bunting and Linnet in winter. Further west extend the rice-paddies of Isla Menor, the area of agricultural land lying between the river Guadalquivir and its tributary, El Brazo del Este.

After 12.5 km you will reach another meander (**Stop D**), a good site for a range of new species for the itinerary such as Purple Heron, Great Crested and Little Grebes, Black-winged Stilt and Avocet.

Once past the meander you will notice next to the track a shallow but broad canal that is one of the best spots in Doñana for Marbled Duck; here too, you may come across Zitting Cisticola and even Great Bittern.

Continue on to 14.0 km and a large meander known as Capitán for the final halt (**Stop E**). Listen out for Savi's Warbler, Reed Bunting or, during migration periods, Water Pipit and enjoy the courtship of the Marsh Harriers and the coming and goings of the Penduline Tits in the bulrushes. The nearby eucalyptus, full of House Sparrows, are also used by Common Kestrels and other raptors, and the exposed patches of mud are frequented by Kentish Plover and the shy Jack Snipe.

Continuing even further south surrounded by more rice-paddies, check the fields for wintering birds of prey such as Short-eared Owl, Merlin and the elegant Hen Harrier. After 16.0 km you reach a asphalted road with on the left the Pinzón pumping station and on the right, a large silo known as El Reboso (Arroceros del Bajo Guadalquivir, Sociedad Cooperativa Andaluza El Reboso). Here ends Itinerary 19 and you can return to your staring point again by turning left and following the asphalt north-east towards Los Palacios y Villafranca.

PRACTICAL GUIDE

Other access points: If you are travelling towards Seville on the N-IV you cannot turn off at km point 568.8 and you must continue as far as the town of Los Palacios y Villafranca and then turn round and head back towards Cádiz. Alternatively, head straight for the settlements of Chapatales and Pinzón from one of the roundabouts in the town.

Additional information: Despite being a protected area, this site has no infrastructure for birdwatchers. The extensive network of *muros* (raised embankments that act as tracks) make getting around easy and are ideal places birdwatching. The official name of this site is Paraje Natural Brazo del Este and is part of the Andalusian network of protected spaces. It has also been recently declared a RAMSAR site.

Transport: In winter take care after rain and we recommend that you begin the route at the end and continue as far as the state of the tracks allows. There are petrol stations open 24 hours a day in Los Palacios y Villafranca. There is no public transport.

Water and toilets: In Pinzón and Chapatales there are bars where you can eat, buy water and use the toilets. Los Palacios y Villafranca has a wide range of supermarkets and restaurants.

Wheelchair access: There are no complications for wheelchair users since all the stops are in areas with broad, well-made tracks. Mud in the wet season may, however, be somewhat of a problem.

Recommendation: See the recommendations from the previous itinerary.

Itinerary nº 20

FROM TREBUJENA TO THE MONTE ALGAIDA SALTPANS

Carretera del Práctico

BASIC INFORMATION

Start: Trebujena (29S 751427 4084628)
End: Hide at Monte Algaida saltpans (29S 736885 4084591)
Distance: 17 km by vehicle and 0.7 km on foot
Maps: SGE 11-43 and 12-43 (1:50,000)
Municipalities: Trebujena and Sanlúcar de Barrameda (Cádiz)

The whole area between the river Guadalquivir and the towns of Lebrija and Trebujena once formed part of the south-eastern Guadalquivir salt-marshes. Over the last 100 years the drainage of the salt-marshes to provide land for agriculture and stock-raising has led to the construction of endless canals, embankments and sluice-gates and today this area is no longer tidal and only floods after heavy rain. The river Guadalquivir, however, acts as a conduit between the dried out salt-marshes and the saltpans of Monte Algaida, where water remains all year round, and a wealth of birdlife is attracted to this area by the lack of disturbance, mild climate and abundant food.

DESCRIPTION

Begin the itinerary in the town of Trebujena, having come from the neighbouring town of Lebrija. Enter Trebujena and at the first roundabout, turn right uphill along 'Avda. del Guadalquivir' as far as 'Ronda de Palomares', a road that will take you out of the town towards the river Guadalquivir. When you reach a school – 'Instituto de Enseñanza Secundaria Alventus' – reset your kilometre counter.

At first you pass through vineyards set in a rolling landscape, where Barn Owls call on spring evenings and the vast *marisma* lies ahead on the horizon. As you begin to drop the meanders of

Monte Algaida saltpans © Jorge Garzón

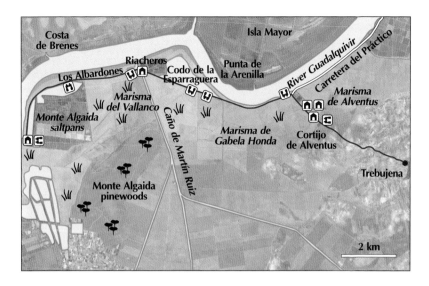

the Guadalquivir come into view, only to disappear as you reach a plain known as Marisma de Alventus and a farm of the same name (3.6 km). This is an excellent site in winter for large flocks of Northern Lapwing and European Golden Plover. After 4.8 km you will come to a tourist accommodation with traditional Doñana-style huts and then just a little way ahead you reach the badly maintained Carretera del Práctico, an asphalted road named after the stevedores who once travelled along here from Seville to Sanlúcar de Barrameda to work. Turn left and head downstream alongside the Guadalquivir.

La Carretera del Práctico or 'del Plástico', as it is referred to locally, runs parallel to the river Guadalquivir on your right; on the left, the wide open spaces of Marisma de Gabela Honda are still reasonably well preserved. After 6.0 km reach **Stop A**. The salt-marsh vegetation here of saltworts and glassworts is ideal for birds such as the shy Spectacled Warbler, Lesser

The slope of the land is inappreciable in the salt-marshes   © Jesús Martín

Avocet © Javier Ramos

Short-toed Lark – who love to dust-bathe in the tracks – and Pin-tailed Sandgrouse.

Stop B comes after 10 km from the start of the itinerary, next to the open waters of Codo de la Esparraguera. This water body always provides good observations and is a sure site for Greater Flamingo, Grey Heron, Yellow-legged Gull, Common Coot, Little Grebe and, sometimes, the scarce White-headed Duck.

From here you will reach Cooperativa de Riacheros in 1.3 km, where the small fishing boats that ply these waters for prawns and eels find harbour. Cross a small bridge over El Caño de Martín Ruiz (now converted into a canal) and immediately afterwards, turn right to a hide located next to a sharp bend in the track where the asphalt runs out. Here at 11.7 km park (**Stop C**) and try and spot four of the *Tringa* species of wader (or 'shanks') that frequent Doñana: Common and Spotted Redshanks, Greenshank and Marsh Sandpiper. Green Sandpipers and Zitting Cisticola move around the moored boats and during spring migration Grasshopper Warblers sing from the nearby reeds.

Continue south-east along the track, still parallel to the river, with Marisma del Vallanco, a vast extension of saltworts and glassworts, and the Algaida pinewoods away to the east. Pay attention to the tidal mud between the track and the river (Los Albardones), which can be very productive for plovers and sandpipers, and the newly 'planted' dead trees, which have become a favourite place for Ospreys to rest or to tear up a recently caught fish. Another one of the star species in this sector of Doñana is the Marbled Duck, while one of our personal favourite spots near here are the tidal salt-marshes, where pipit and wagtail migration gives a good idea of how the year's passerine migration is faring. Here we expect to see, in order of abundance, the *ibe-riae*, *flava* and *flavissima* subspecies of the Yellow Wagtail.

After almost 14 km of solid surface, the good track begins to run out and you begin a stretch of clayey track where you must take care during the rainy season. Ahead two tracks run parallel to each other: the higher of the two offers better views, but is narrower and less even. Just 1 km further on you will see on the other side of the river Casa de Brenes, the point where the three provinces of Doñana – Seville, Huelva and Cádiz – meet. After a total of 15 km, stop next to Monte Algaida (**Stop D**) and scan the tracts of salt-marsh vegetation (saltworts and glass-

PRACTICAL GUIDE

Other access points: You can reach the observation point at Monte Algaida and follow the itinerary backwards by starting at Stop B of Itinerary 21 (after 5 km of sinuous tracks only accessible by 4WD vehicles).

Additional information: The *marismas* of Alventus and Vallanco are not protected and are under pressure from developers and so could disappear under concrete at any moment. From El Caño de Martín Ruiz onwards you are in the Doñana Natural Park and the only visitor infrastructures are the precarious observation points mentioned in the text. The nearest visitor centre is La Fábrica del Hielo in the town of Sanlúcar de Barrameda. All the tracks are public.

Transport: There are no real difficulties in this itinerary, although be careful on the tracks and especially on the potholed Carretera del Práctico. Trebujena is connected to Sanlúcar de Barrameda, Cádiz, Lebrija and Seville by public transport, although no bus route actually connects to this itinerary. Trebujena and Sanlúcar de Barrameda have petrol stations open 24 hours a day.

Water and toilets: There is no water available on this itinerary and the only public toilet is in the canteen of the Cooperativa de Riacheros.

Wheelchair access: In general wheelchair access is fine and there are no special problems at any of the stopping or observations points. Only mud in the rainy season and the sandy track at the last stop could cause a few problems.

Recommendation: The final 700 m of the itinerary are on sandy soil and could be problematical for some vehicles. We therefore recommend you walk this last section. This is an excellent itinerary to follow in the afternoon owing to the position of the sun. Telescopes are all but essential to view the wide open areas and mosquito repellent a must at nightfall.

In Lebrija there is a Lesser Kestrel colony in the town church and a visit will allow you to appreciate the life of a colony of this beautiful but threatened species.

Group of Eurasian Spoonbills   © Jesús Martín

worts) and saltpans for migrants. As well, you may come across Common Shelduck, Black-necked Grebe, Eurasian Spoonbill, Great Egret and Red-knobbed Coot, while on the small ridges between the saltpans Eurasian Curlew, Whimbrel and Grey and other Plovers rest and feed.

After 17.7 km you reach a viewing point consisting of fence overlooking the saltpans: this spot marks the end of this itinerary (**Stop E**) and a good site at dusk for finding shy rails such as Water Rail and Spotted Crake.

Also here, look out for feeding Black-winged Stilts, Avocets, Black-tailed Godwits and Black and Whiskered Terns. From the right of the observation point a path takes you to the river Guadalquivir and amazing views over into the dunes and pine forests of the Doñana National Park. If you end up here at dusk, there still might just have time to witness the powerful flight of the Spanish Imperial Eagle; for those who choose to stay even later in the day, the reflection of the moonlight on the peaceful waters of the 'Río Grande' will provide a chance to reflect on the sheer beauty of this corner of the globe.

Itinerary nº 21

THE BONANZA SALTPANS AND LA ALGAIDA PINEWOOD
San Carlos saltpans and Laguna de Tarelo

BASIC INFORMATION

Start: Gate to Bonanza saltpans (29S 737667 4078805)
End: Hide at Laguna de Tarelo (29S 739460 4081465)
Distance: 4.5 km by vehicle and 0.5 km on foot
Maps: SGE 11-43 and 11-44 (1:50,000)
Municipalities: Sanlúcar de Barrameda (Cádiz)

Whereas in the previous itinerary you could sniff the Atlantic on the sea breeze, in this itinerary you come all but face to face with the sea. Away over on the far shore of the mighty river Guadalquivir the virgin expanses of the National Park stretch invitingly.

Maritime Doñana begins in Bajo de Guía, the waterside quarter of the lovely town of Sanlúcar de Barrameda. This itinerary is split into two parts: the first

Bonanza saltpans   © Jorge Garzón

visits the saltpans, while the second heads for the pine woods and ends up at a very important wetland, Laguna de Tarelo.

DESCRIPTION

To start, pick up the road that heads for 'Puerto de Bonanza' and 'Colonia agrícola de La Algaida', an agricultural estate. This road is the continuation of 'Puerto de Barrameda', a street in the Bajo de Guía district. Almost immediately the feel of the saltpans envelopes you as you see ahead the first mountains of salt. After passing the salt works of APROMASA and PROA SAL you should take a track off left signposted Salinas de Bonanza (noting the sign right to Pinar de la Algaida). Following the left-hand track for 1 km you reach the entrance gate to the saltpans, the starting point of this itinerary and where you should reset your kilometre counter. Despite a no-entry sign, the gate is always open and the owners

have no objections to vehicles entering into the saltpans provided that no nuisance is caused.

The main track is surrounded at first by crystallising tanks where the salt precipitates out. Here you should look for a small pumping station on the right side of the track (**Stop A**; 0.8 km), a perfect site for viewing the sheets of open water and searching for the most interesting species. You will have no problems finding one of the most assiduous visitors to the saltpans, the Slender-billed Gull, while the small embankments between the tanks are a favourite place for Caspian and raucous Little Terns and Mediterranean and Audouin's Gulls. Here too we have come across a vagrant Ring-billed Gull.

Continue along the same track with a line of electricity posts on your left as far as a T-junction, from where you will have no problems spotting the striking plumage of the groups of Common Shelduck that frequent this area

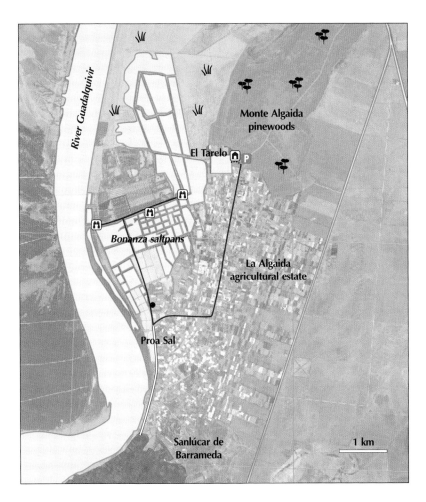

River Guadalquivir

Monte Algaida pinewoods

El Tarelo   P

Bonanza saltpans

La Algaida agricultural estate

Proa Sal

Sanlúcar de Barrameda

1 km

of the saltpans. Turn left towards the river Guadalquivir and reach a sign reading 'Acuinova San Carlos' (**Stop B**; 1,8 km), where you should halt to look for two more species of terns, Sandwich and Common, as well as Kentish Plovers running around the salt-marsh vegetation. Other vociferous denizens of this sector of the saltpans are Common Redshanks, Common Sandpipers incessantly patrolling the canals, and the Kingfishers that sit on the nearby

Group of resting Kentish Plovers   © Mario Martín

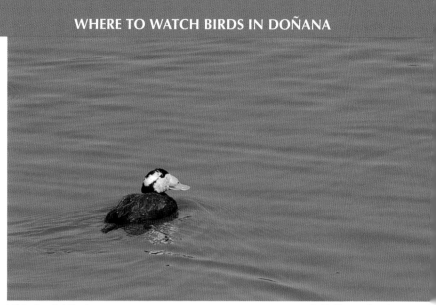

White-headed Duck © Guillermo Garzón

La Algaida pinewoods © Francisco Chiclana

sluice-gates. Walk to the river to appreciate the full beauty of the pine forests of the National Park on the far bank; from here you will have views of the traditional settlement of La Plancha and with luck of mammals such as Red and Fallow Deer and Wild Boar.

Return to the T-junction and continue straight on alongside a canal with the power line to your right. After 2.4 km (**Stop C**) stop to investigate the evaporation tanks where waders such as Curlew Sandpiper, Sanderling, Turnstone, Avocet, Black-tailed and Bartailed Godwits, Curlew and Whimbrel are regular visitors. During migration periods this is a good spot too for Red-necked Phalarope.

Continue as far as a small white hut (another pumping station) at the edge of a large open sheet of water holding at times hundreds, if not thousands, of feeding Greater Flamingoes (**Stop D**; 3 km). Many more waders

feed here: look for the Knot and Spotted Redshank whose colouration depends on the time of year. This area of the saltpans is tidal and you will have better fortune looking for waders at low tide. Other frequent visitors to the saltpans here include the voracious Yellow-legged Gull and Common Ravens, whose deep croaks will reveal their presence.

To continue on to the pine forest you must leave the saltpans via the same entrance gate and return to the sign reading 'Pinar de la Algaida', where you should reset your kilometre counter and continue left along the asphalted road with the PROA SAL salt works on your right. Continue along the Carretera de Bonanza, surrounded by plastic greenhouses and small market gardens. Once at the pine forest (4.5 km), park and continue on foot to Laguna de Tarelo (**Stop E**) and its hide. 'Algaida' means woods or stands of

PRACTICAL GUIDE

Additional information: Apart from part of La Laguna de Tarelo, all of this area lies within the Doñana Natural Park, although there are no visitor centres or any other infrastructure for birdwatchers. The nearest visitor centre is La Fábrica de Hielo in Sanlúcar de Barrameda. An added attraction in the area are the archaeological remains of the Turdetanian culture.

Transport: This is an easy itinerary to follow. Sanlúcar de Barrameda is well connected by public transport and there is a regular bus between the town and La Colonia de Algaida that will drop you at the start and finish of this itinerary. Remember that the saltpans are private and that you must drive responsibly when inside and not leave the main track. In Sanlúcar de Barrameda there are petrol stations that stay open 24 hours a day.

Water and toilets: Water and toilets are available in the bars and restaurants of Sanlúcar de Barrameda.

Wheelchair access: Access in wheelchairs is generally reasonably good and there are no particular problems at any of the stops or in the hide. The Cerro del Águila is too sandy for wheelchairs.

Recommendation: Any time of the day is good as you can always look away from the sun. Insect repellent is essential in the pine woods and at the lagoon. The pine forest is home to an interesting population of the Mediterranean Chameleon (*Chamaeleo chamaeleon*).

trees near water courses and comes from the Arab 'al-gaidah' ('the wood').

From the comfort of the hide begin to look for the most emblematic of Doñana's diving ducks, the White-headed Duck, in the best place for the species in the area. It rarely swims alone and is almost always accompanied by Black-necked Grebes, Tufted Duck, Common Pochard and Pintail. To the right of the hide a path – Cerro del Águila – heads off for a five-kilometre walk through the pines, the best way to find some of the area's most interesting diurnal and nocturnal raptors: Black and Red Kites, Short-toed Eagle and Tawny and Long-eared Owls. Keep an eye out for Azure-winged Magpie, for this is the only site in the whole of the province of Cádiz for this member of the Crow family. This umbrella pine forest also has an interesting contingent of migrant and resident passerines that include Iberian and Common Chiffchaffs and Willow Warbler, as well as numerous Common Chaffinches, as rare to the east of the Guadalquivir as they are common to the west.

Itinerary nº 22

THE BEACHES OF MONTIJO AND LA JARA
The mouth of the river Guadalquivir

BASIC INFORMATION
Start and end: Montijo beach (29S 731805 4071673)
Distance: 6 km on foot
Map: SGE 11-44 (scale 1:50,000)
Municipalities: Chipiona and Sanlúcar de Barrameda (Cádiz)

Many birdwatchers who visit Doñana are unaware of the possibilities offered by the coast between Chipiona and Sanlúcar de Barrameda and so this itinerary explores this coastal strip with its stunning views over the mouth of the river Guadalquivir and away across to the idyllic sands of the Doñana itself.

The itinerary is dominated by the collision of the broad waters of the river Guadalquivir with the mighty Atlantic. This estuary is of great importance

Playa de Montijo at low tide   © Jorge Garzón

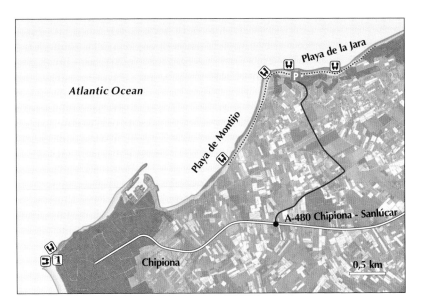

and the mixing of the fresh water of the river and the saline waters of the ocean provide rich pickings in the form of small fish and invertebrates for many thousands of birds. The river is also an important two-way migration corridor and acts as the entrance gate into the heart of the Doñana.

A visit to the site of the lighthouse at Chipiona – at 68 metres the tallest in Spain – is a must since this magnificent lookout point offers the best seawatching possibilities anywhere on the Doñana coastline.

DESCRIPTION

Begin the itinerary on the beach of Playa de Montijo: take the A-480 from Sanlúcar de Barrameda towards Chipiona and just after km point 2.0, turn right at a roundabout as indicated to 'Montijo'. Just 1.3 km further ahead you will see signs for 'CIFA Chipiona' and 'Corrales de pesca Chipiona', at which point you should turn left. Continue on to Venta Aurelio, park and head for the beach either straight on or to the right along any of the paths that pass behind the houses and allotments.

Playa de Montijo lies within the municipality of Chipiona and still boasts a number of *corrales*, long stone walls used to trap fish and shellfish as the tides rise and fall that are of Arab origin. There are no specific stops during this itinerary and birdwatchers should pause wherever they see fit.

Walk west along the sand amongst pebbles and seaweed and head towards Playa de la Jara through an ideal area for birds who feed on marine invertebrates. Kentish Plovers in the company of Curlew Sandpiper, Knot and Sanderling, three species of wader whose plumage varies with the seasons, will accompany you during the first part of the walk. Although binoculars will provide good enough views, you really ought to have a telescope with you here to enjoy the full repertoire of birds that frequent this beach. Grey Plover watch as long-billed waders such as Bar-tailed Godwit, Whimbrel and Eurasian Curlew probe the mud

Lighhouse and shallows at Chipiona   © Francisco Chiclana

for the worms that are their main source of nutrition.

Away on the other side of the river extends the beaches of Doñana. Gulls begin to appear: the commonest are Yellow-legged and Slender-billed Gulls, whilst the rarest tend to be Mediterranean, Audouin's and Great Black-backed Gulls. On the beach Turnstones act in character by searching under pebbles and shells for food, Oyster-catchers stand out from the surrounding rocks and, out to sea, Caspian Terns plummet into the sea in search of fish against a background of a grounded cargo ship.

Terns are also well in evidence here and take advantage of the broad inter-tidal zone to rest. Groups of Little Terns are common and you should also scan the groups of Sandwich and Common Terns for an unexpected surprise in the shape of Royal, Lesser Crested or Arctic Tern.

Almost without realising, you reach Playa de la Jara in Sanlúcar de Barra-meda, historically famous as the point where Magellan and Elcano's first ever

Slender-billed Gull   © José Antonio Sencianes

Bar-tailed Godwit   © José Antonio Lama

circumnavigation of the globe began in 1519 and then finished three years later.

Retrace you steps to your vehicle and head for the nearby town of Chipiona, where you should find your way to the lighthouse whose glow is visible over much of Doñana at night. Set up your observation point just below the light-house on a small esplanade and begin seawatching. You will not be disappointed as this site provides good views of Northern Gannets of all ages, Balearic and Cory's Shearwaters riding the waves and rafts of Common Scoter. During migration periods look out for the fragile flight of the Atlantic Puffin, Common Guillemot and Razorbill,

PRACTICAL GUIDE

Other access points: You can reach the start of this itinerary from Sanlúcar de Barrameda or Chipiona.

Additional information: This site is unprotected other than by the laws that the Ministry of the Environment enforces on the whole of the coastline. There is no infrastructure for birdwatchers; all the paths are public.

Transport: You can reach the beginning of the itinerary on foot from the marina in Chipiona or from the centre of Sanlúcar de Barrameda. Vehicles are forbidden on the sand. There is no bus-stop at the start of the itinerary, but access is easy from the nearby towns.

Water and toilets: You should carry water as the public drinking fountains and toilets on the beach are often closed.

Wheelchair access: Access to the beach is not problematical, but the sandy beach may be impractical for wheelchairs.

Recommendation: Try to walk this itinerary at low tide as the rocky platform and sand exposed at low tide attracts many birds to feed.

joined after westerly storms by European and Leach's Storm-petrels.

Another attraction is the zigzagging flight of the Great and Arctic Skuas that patrol these waters in search of a gull or tern to pursue and force to relinquish its most recent capture. Pay attention to any small stubby birds in flight as not far from here there is a colony of Little Swifts.

If you can, stay until sunset and enjoy the views over to the clear virgin sands of Doñana crowned by the dark pinewoods, while cargo ships begin the haul upriver to Seville watchful of the dangerous sandbanks that adorn the estuary. Unsurprisingly, the first signal light erected here was built as long ago as 140 AD to safeguard the passage of the Roman ships bringing supplies from afar.

Itinerary nº 23

THE MARSHES OF TREBUJENA
The Monteagudo marshland

BASIC INFORMATION
Start: Km point 51.8 of the A-471 (29S 744560 4075828)
End: Road A-471 (29S 743102 4073848)
Distance: 8.4 km by vehicle and 2.4 km on foot
Map: SGE 11-44 (scale 1:50,000)
Municipalities: Sanlúcar de Barrameda (Cádiz)

Between Cortijo de Alventus and El Cerro de Évora in Sanlúcar de Barrameda lies a plain that is home to some of Doñana's best steppe birds; the area

The marshes of Trebujena   © Jorge Garzón

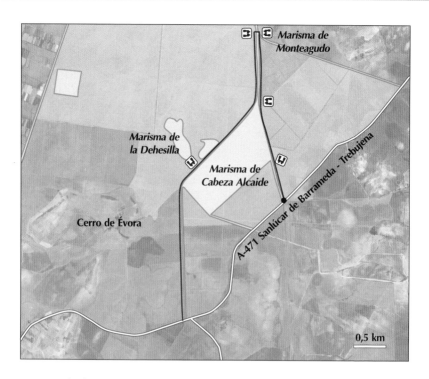

consists of a drained salt-marsh partially transformed into agricultural land and grazing that still retains patches of saltwort and other halophyte plants. These fields, overlooked by the low hill of Cerro de Monteagudo, were home not so long ago to Doñana's last Great Bustards.

The thousand faces of Doñana are represented no better than here, where the vagaries of the local climate in wet years can transform this plain into a marsh frequented by thousands of waders, gulls and other birds.

DESCRIPTION

From Trebujena head towards Sanlúcar de Barrameda along the A-471, keeping a close eye on the kilometre posts: just after passing Cerro de Monteagudo, at km point 51.8 pick up a track off to the right and head into the salt-marshes. Reset your kilometre counter to zero.

The immensity of the vast plain opens out in front of you. Despite seeming at first somewhat devoid of life, it is important to be aware that many of the birds you are searching for hide in the small depressions that abound in this far from flat extension of land. Just 800 m from the start stop next to a fence (**Stop A**), whose posts are favourites perching sites for Common Kestrel, Common Buzzard and Hoopoes. Above you, Common, Pallid and Alpine Swifts share the airspace.

Continue northwards, noting the different types of salt-marsh vegetation. To your left species of genera *Salicornia* and *Sarcocornia* dominate, while to your right in the rather drier areas *Suaeda* and *Arthrocnemum* are the predominant plants and attract many of the site's steppe birds. After 1.5 km (**Stop B**) stop next to a cattle enclosure and a metal fence and use

Red-legged Partridge © José Manuel Reyes

your telescopes to look for the cryptically coloured Pin-tailed Sandgrouse and Stone Curlew. It will be rather easier to locate by their songs the Crested and Lesser Short-toed Larks that coexist here, while from the top of a low bush the Spectacled Warbler emits its harsh call. Red-legged Partridges and Quail fly off low and deceptively quickly when disturbed.

After 3.1 km, you reach a T-junction (**Stop C**) where you should climb any of the earth mounds to get a better view of the surrounding fields. Look out for the low flight of Montagu's Harrier, especially common during migration periods, the rapid flight of the Barn Swallow along the canals, the nervous sallies of the Tawny Pipit and differing postures of the Northern and Black-eared Wheatears.

From here you can park and continue on foot to the right into the interesting ecosystems of the Monteagudo salt-marshes. Check out the fields and low scrub for three species of wader: Northern Lapwing, European Golden Plover and with luck a group of the scarce Dotterel mixed in with the previous two species. Return to the vehicle as you see fit and continue ahead.

Continue left and cross a broad canal on a three-arched bridge and begin to head more or less south on the other side of the *caño* (channel). After 3.5 km the asphalt runs out and the track turns sharp right: however, you should continue straight on alongside the channel. After 5.5 km, make the final stop (**Stop D**) of this itinerary next to a solitary tamarisk, from where you may disturb some young Woodchat Shrikes. Even with your telescope will you find it difficult to take in the whole vastness of the Dehesilla

Yellow Wagtail   © Diego López

salt-marshes. Concentrate on the many large stones scattered around the plains, the favourite perches of wintering Merlin, and look out for the graceful silhouette of the Hobby, which we have seen here even in winter (January 2005).

You may end up spending hours here searching the horizon for other species, although you can be sure of seeing Yellow Wagtail. Continue along the track with Cerro de Évora to your right and its fields of cereals and sunflowers frequented by Linnets and Corn Buntings.

After 8.5 km you reach the A-471 again and the end of this itinerary.

PRACTICAL GUIDE

Other access points: The beginning of this itinerary can be reached easily from Trebujena, Sanlúcar de Barrameda and Jerez de la Frontera.

Additional information: This site is unprotected, although much is classified as priority habitats by the Habitats Directive, which thus obliges the Andalusian Government to implement some kind of protection. There is no infrastructure for birdwatchers; all tracks are public.

Transport: This itinerary is easy to follow other than after heavy rain, when some parts of the track may become impassable. There is no official bus-stop at the starting point to the itinerary. There are petrol stations open all day in Trebujena and Sanlúcar de Barrameda. Near the end of the itinerary there is a petrol station open during the day.

Water and toilets: You should carry water from the start as there are no water sources or toilets anywhere on the itinerary.

Wheelchair access: In general wheelchair access is possible although after rain mud may be a problem.

Recommendation: Follow this itinerary in a reverse sense in the afternoon. At dusk the salt-marshes take on surreal colours that will delight photographers. Stay in or next to your vehicle to avoid disturbing birds with your silhouette.

Other titles available:

- *Atles dels ocells nidificants de Catalunya 1999-2002* [J. Estrada, V. Pedrocchi, Ll. Brotons & S. Herrando]
- *Grebes of our World* (A. Konter)
- *El lince ibérico.* [J. Pérez de Albéniz]
- *The Spanish Imperial Eagle* (M. Ferrer)
- *Ecology and Conservation of Steppe-land Birds* (G. Bota, M. B. Morales, S. Mañosa & J. Camprodon)
- *Las aves marinas de España y Portugal* (A. Paterson)
- *Guía de las cajas nido y comederos para aves y otros vertebrados* (J. Baucells, J. Camprodon, J. Cerdeira & P. Vila)
- *Parques Nacionales de España, 26 itinerarios para descubrirlos y conocerlos* (O. Alamany & E. Vicens)
- *Itineraris pels parcs naturals de Catalunya* (J. Bas, A. Curcó & J. Orta)
- *On observar ocells a Catalunya* (14 authors)
- *Catàleg dels ocells dels Països Catalans* (J. Clavell)
- *Where to watch birds in Spain. The best 100 sites* (J. A. Montero)
- *A Birdwatcher's Guide to Italy* (L. Ruggieri & I. Festari)
- *Birding in Venezuela* (M. L. Goodwin)
- *Aves de España* (E. de Juana & J. M. Varela)
- *Guía sonora de las aves de Europa* (10 CDs; J. Roché & J. Chevereau)
- *Guía de las aves de O Caurel* (J. Guitián, I. Munilla, M. González & M. Arias)
- *A Field Guide to the Birds of Peru* (J. F. Clements & N. Shany; colour drawings by D. Gardner & E. Barnes)
- *Birds of South Asia: the Ripley Guide* (P. C. Rasmussen & J. C. Anderton)
- *Annotated Checklist of the Birds of Argentina* (J. Mazar Barnett & M. Pearman)
- *Annotated Checklist of the Birds of Belize* (H. Lee Jones & A. C. Vallely)
- *Annotated Checklist of the Birds of Chile* (M. Marín)
- *Mamíferos de España* (F. J. Purroy & J. M. Varela)
- *Arte de pájaros / Art of Birds* (P. Neruda)
- *Threatened Birds of the World* (BirdLife International)
- *Curassows and Related Birds. Second Edition* (J. Delacour & D. Amadon)
- *Handbook of the Birds of the World* (J. del Hoyo, A. Elliott, D. Christie & J. Sargatal)
  Vol. 1: Ostrich to Ducks
  Vol. 2: New World Vultures to Guineafowl
  Vol. 3: Hoatzin to Auks
  Vol. 4: Sandgrouse to Cuckoos
  Vol. 5: Barn-owls to Hummingbirds
  Vol. 6: Mousebirds to Hornbills
  Vol. 7: Jacamars to Woodpeckers
  Vol. 8: Broadbills to Tapaculos
  Vol. 9: Cotingas to Pipits and Wagtails
  Vol. 10: Cuckoo-shrikes to Thrushes
- Wildlife Travel Maps of Spain. Catalonia (1/300,000)
- Wildlife Travel Maps of Spain. Balearic Islands (1/150,000)
- Wildlife Travel Maps of Spain. Extremadura (1/300,000)

For more information, please visit our website:
www.hbw.com

Montseny, 8, 08193 - Bellaterra, Barcelona (Spain)
Tel: (+34) 93 594 77 10 / Fax: (+34) 93 592 09 69
E-mail: lynx@hbw.com